Fifth Grade Math

For Home School or Extra Practice

By Greg Sherman

Home School Brew Press

www.HomeSchoolBrew.com

Printed in the United States of America

Table of Contents

Disclaimer

This book was developed for parents and students of no particular state; while it is based on common core standards, it is always best to check with your state board to see what will be included on testing.

About Us

Homeschool Brew was started for one simple reason: to make affordable Homeschooling books! When we began looking into homeschooling our own children, we were astonished at the cost of curriculum. Nobody ever said homeschool was easy, but we didn't know that the cost to get materials would leave us broke.

We began partnering with educators and parents to start producing the same kind of quality content that you expect in expensive books...but at a price anyone can afford.

We are still in our infancy stages, but we will be adding more books every month. We value your feedback, so if you have any comments about what you like or how we can do better, then please let us know!

To add your name to our mailing list, go here: http://www.homeschoolbrew.com/mailing-list.html

Algebra

Algebra is a part of math in which letters are substituted for numbers. Algebra uses both letters and numbers to create equations. In math, there are ways to represent relationship between numbers. One very common type of relationship is a linear relationship. A linear relationship is when one side of an equation equals the other side of the equation and is represented by a linear equation. A linear equation has a variable, such as x or y.

For example, $x + 3 = 8$

It is important to understand that in a linear equation, one side MUST equal the other side. When working with a linear equation, it does not matter how many variables are in the equation or what operations the equation includes, the sides will always be equal.

Equations

An equation is a mathematic sentence. An equation says that two things are equal. An equal sign is always used in an equation. An example of an arithmetic equation is $3 + 5 = 8$. The left side $(3 + 5)$ is equal to the right side (8). In an equation, both sides must always be equal. An example of an algebraic equation is $3 + x = 8$. The left side $(3 + x)$ is equal to the right side (8). In the algebraic equation, the value of x could be substituted for a number that would make the equation true and make both sides equal.

In an equation, many different operations can be used. There can be addition, subtraction, multiplication and division. There could also be exponents or parentheses. It may be necessary to use the order of operations to solve equations.

There are times when you may be given some information and you need to figure the rest of the information out on your own. For example, you know how much it costs to buy 1 item, but you need to figure out how much it will cost you to buy 6 items. An equation will be able to help you figure out the problem. In situations where you may not have all of the information you need, you can use what is called a variable to help you.

Variables

A variable is a symbol that represents something else. Variables represent a number or value that is unknown. The most common symbols used for variables are "x" and "y." The value of the symbol changes based on the problem that it is in. For example:

$C = v \times 4$

In this problem, C is the total cost, 4 is how much it costs to buy a bag of chips and v is the variable. If you want to purchase 5 bags of chips, you could substitute the v for 5. You would then be able to figure out that $5 \times 4 = 20$ and you would be spending $20 for 5 bags of chips. If you want to purchase 8 bags of chips, you could substitute the v for 8. You would then be able to figure out that $8 \times 4 = 32$ and you would be spending $32 for 8 bags of chips.

When you are faced with a mathematical problem in which all of the numbers or values are not known, you will need to use a variable to represent that unknown value or values.

For example, there are 7 children in the neighborhood. Three of the children are girls. The other children are boys. How many boys are there? You do not know the value of the number of boys, so you would represent that value with a variable such as x. You would then represent this equation as $7 = x + 3$.

Variables are used in equations. An equation is a statement about numbers. For example:

$3 + 2 = 2 + 3$ or $4 + x = x + 4$

Representing a Variable

Variables can be represented in a number of different ways. Variables can be represented as a box □. However, variables are most often represented as a letter. Some of the common letters that are used for variables are: x, y, n, t, a, b, c. Letters are often used to represent a variable because a letter can stand for something. In the case of the bags of chips, you could have represented the total cost as T and the cost of the bag of chips as c for chips. The letter x is the most commonly used variable as x often stands for unknown.

Using letters to represent variables saves space and gives you much more freedom to represent the problem in the way that makes sense to you.

Using Variables

Variables should be treated the same as numbers despite the fact that they are letters. They should be treated this way because they represent a number. For example:

$2 + x = 5$ should be treated the same as $2 + 3 = 5$

When a variable is being added or subtracted it will be represented as $x + 4$ or $x - 4$. You should then add the variable or subtract the variable just as you would a number.

When a variable is being multiplied it will be represented as $2x$ or $2(x)$. When a variable is being divided it will be represented as $x/2$.

You should then multiply the variable or divide the variable just as you would a number.

Solving Equations

When solving equations, the most important thing is getting the variable by itself!

Step 1: Identify the variable

Step 2: Identify the operation

Step 3: Identify the opposite of the operation (for example, the opposite of addition is subtraction)

Step 4: Use the opposite operation to move the number on the same side as the variable to the other side of the equal sign

Step 5: If there is a number attached to the variable, move that number to the other side of the equal sign using the opposite operation

Step 6: Write the answer to the equation as the variable = the answer

One-step equations are equations that have one variable and one operation.

For example, $x + 5 = 10$ or $2x = 6$

In the example $x + 5 = 10$, x is the only variable and addition is the only operation. In the example $2x = 6$, x is the only variable and 2 is being multiplied to x. After identifying the variable and the operation, identify the opposite of the operation. The opposite of addition is subtraction.

To solve a one-step equation, the x must be isolated, or be by itself on one side.

$x + 5 = 10$

To get the x by itself, you must move the 5 from the left side of the equation to the right side of the equation. To do that, do the opposite of addition, which is subtraction. Subtract 5 from both sides.

$x + 5 = 10$

$-5 \quad -5$

That leaves you with $x = 5$

To solve the equation $2x = 6$, you must get the x by itself. Identify x as the only variable and the operation as multiplication. Since the 2 is being multiplied to x, the only way to move it is to do the opposite operation, which is to divide both sides by 2.

$2x = 6$

--- ---

2 2

That leaves you with $x = 3$

Two- step equations are equations that have more than one operation. When solving a two-step equation, it is still most important to get the variable by itself.

$2x - 4 = 4$

In this example, the two operations are subtraction and multiplication. After identifying the variable as x and the two operations, figure out the opposite of the operations. The opposite of subtraction is addition and the opposite of multiplication is division.

Always start by moving the number that is not closest to or attached to the variable. Start by adding 4 to both sides.

$2x - 4 = 4$

+4   +4

That leaves $2x = 8$. To get the variable by itself, do the opposite of multiplication which means you will divide both sides by 2

$2x = 8$

---- ----

2   2

$x = 4$

Coefficients

A coefficient is a number that is attached to a variable. For example, 3y or 8x. Coefficients are being multiplied to the variable. In an equation, showing multiplication as $3 \times y$ or $8 \times x$ would be confusing. It would be very easy to mistake a multiplication sign for an x. To simplify, coefficients are used.

Whenever a number and a variable are attached, that means that the variable is being multiplied to the number. That is very important to remember for when you are identifying the opposite operation. Any time you see a coefficient, remember that the opposite is division.

When identifying a coefficient, always look at the number in front of the variable. A coefficient could be a one digit number or a five digit number. There may be numbers after a variable or the variable may be squared or cubed. Those operations or numbers do not change what the coefficient is.

For example, $34x^2$, the coefficient is 34

Exercises

1. Owen has 31 cousins. 17 of his cousins are boys. He wants to figure out how many of his cousins are girls. Which equation represents the situation?

   $31 = x \times 17$ $\quad\quad$ $31 = x - 17$ $\quad\quad$ $31 = x + 17$

2. What is the variable in the equation $90 - 10 = r$? ______

3. Solve for the variable: $24 \div x = 4$ ______

4. I am an equation that uses the letter z as a variable. I help to find the answer to 90 - 30. Who am I? __________

5. Derek is sailing his ship. He knows that he has gone 130 miles so far. He also knows that he has to sail a total of 189 miles to get where he is going. He wants to know how much further he has to go.

   $189 \times 130 = x$ $\quad\quad$ $189 - 130 = x$ $\quad\quad$ $189 + 130 = x$

6. Solve for the variable: $j + 23 = 44$ ______

7. Ralph is growing pear trees. He has 29 red pear trees and 24 green pear trees. He wants to know how many trees he has all together.

   $29 - 24 = y$ $\quad\quad$ $29 \div 24 = y$ $\quad\quad$ $29 + 24 = y$

8. What is the variable in the equation $11 \times 32 = w$? ______

9. Solve for the variable: $3a = 12$ ______

10. Identify the coefficient: $9y + 18 = 90$ ______

11. Solve for the variable: $b - 12 = 9$ ______

12. I am an equation that uses the letter b as a variable. I help to find the answer to 25 + 4. Who am I?
____

13. Solve for the variable: $5x - 10 = 35$ ______________

14. There are 30 students in your class. You need to split them into 5 teams. Which equation would you use to figure out the students on each team?

$30 - 5 = y$ $30 \div 5 = y$ $30 \times 5 = y$

15. Solve for the variable: $3z + 21 = 51$ _____

16. Identify the coefficient: $125y + 100 = 250$ _____

17. Solve for the variable: $11x - 12 = 43$ _____

18. There are 14 different plants in the garden. Each plant sprouts 8 new buds. Which equation would you use to figure out how many buds you have?

$14 \times 8 = y$ $14 - 8 = y$ $8 - 14 = y$

19. What is the variable in the equation $6p - 25 = 11$? _____

20. Solve for the variable: $10x + 2 = 62$ _____

Quiz

1. Identify the coefficient in the equation $4t - 3 = 5$ ________

2. There are 19 fruit trees in Kyle's backyard. 9 of them are apple trees and the rest are peach trees. Which equation represents the situation?

   $9x = 19$ $\quad$ $9 - x = 19$ $\quad$ $x + 9 = 19$

3. Solve for the variable: $x - 16 = 23$ ________

4. What is the variable in the equation $17 + r = 74$? ________

5. Solve for the variable: $3x + 12 = 36$ ________

6. Identify the coefficient in the equation $20x = 200$ ________

7. Solve for the variable: $5y - 6 = 14$ ________

8. There are 8 kittens in a litter. 3 are black and the rest are white. Which equation represents the situation?

   $3 - x = 8$ $\quad$ $3 + x = 8$ $\quad$ $3x = 8$

9. Solve for the variable: $4x = 16$ ________

10. Solve for the variable: $2x + 9 = 29$ ________

Data Analysis

Data is a collection of values or measurements that is usually gathered by observation or measurement. Data is then generally organized in graphs or charts for analysis.

There are different types of data and each type of data consists of certain types of values. There is data that is collected, analyzed and used immediately. There is also data that is collected, analyzed, used and then published somewhere for others to use. Both types of data are accurate and can be utilized for multiple purposes.

Discrete Data

Discrete data is data that is counted. The data can only take certain values because there are only certain values possible. For example, the number of children in a family can only be a whole number because you cannot have half of a person.

Another example would be that a math quiz is given. There are five questions on the quiz. The number of correct answers on a student's quiz would either be 0, 1, 2, 3, 4 or 5. There are a set number of questions. Therefore, the data is discrete.

Continuous Data

Continuous data is data that is measured. Continuous data can take any value within a specified range. For example, a dog's weight can be any value (within the range of typical weight), not just certain fixed values.

Another example is the height of trees at a nursery. Trees can be any height such as 205.3 centimeters and

580.2 centimeters. The height of the trees does not need to fall within a certain range. Therefore, the data is continuous.

Primary Data

Primary data is data that has been collected first hand. That means that the data has been collected by the person who is going to use it. The data can be collected through surveys, measurements or observations. The data is then immediately used or analyzed.

For example, someone wants to know the number of families who have television sets in their family rooms, so they send a survey to all families in Alberta. That person then collects the surveys, puts the data in a table and uses the data to write an article about modern day families and television use.

Secondary Data

Secondary data is data that has been collected, compiled and published somewhere. Secondary data is then used by someone who did not collect and compile it.

For example, you are interested in finding out how much it has rained for the past year. You know that your local weather station keeps track of how much rain is received each month. You go on their website and find the data on rainfall for each month. You are able to utilize the data that they have already collected and published.

Data Sample

A data sample is taking data from a small group that represents a larger group. Using the tree example, instead of having to take data from every single tree in Canada, you can use a sample of trees across Canada to represent all of the trees.

A data sample is only acceptable if it consists of data from across the area you are collecting data from. Again, using the tree example, you would need to get data from trees across Canada. The data sample would not be acceptable if you only took data from one forest in Canada.

Examples,

You want information on the hair color of all of the 5th grade students in Saskatchewan. You collect data from 5th grade classes all across Saskatchewan.

You need information on the number of squirrels that live in Montreal. You go to several parks throughout Montreal and count the squirrels.

Data Collection

There are a variety of different ways to collect data. Depending on the data needed, sometimes it is possible to measure objects, sometimes it is possible to observe an action and sometimes it is possible to conduct a survey and ask questions. Each of the different methods of data collection is appropriate.

Data collection is the most important step in working with data. Data must be collected using an appropriate method.

Observation

Collecting data using observation is when the person who is need of the data goes to watches and writes down what they see. Observation is the best means of collecting data when you are trying to understand a behavior or a situation (e.g. wanting to see how a dog reacts to a certain toy) or when you want direct information (e.g. wanting to see how cars react to a new stop sign installed).

Measurement

Collecting data using measurement is when the person who is need of the data measures or weighs the object they are looking for data on. Measurement is the best means of collecting data when you are looking for weights, heights, lengths, volume or amounts of something.

Survey

Collecting data using a survey is when the person who is need of the data puts together a group of questions. Those questions are then handed out and people are asked to answer them. Survey is the best means of collecting data when you are trying to gather information on behaviors that are not easily observed (e.g. how often a parent reads to a child throughout the day or how many evenings a family sits down to eat dinner together).

Displaying Data

Data is often displayed in graphs, charts and tables after it is collected so that it can be more easily reviewed and analyzed.

Tables are used to show all data in number form. Tables can contain any number of rows or columns to accommodate all of the data.

For example,

Students in class	Shoe size
Kenny	7
Doris	9
Pamela	13
Douglas	8

Graphs are used to visually represent the data. There are several different types of graphs. Bar graphs and line graphs are the most commonly used types of graphs. Line graphs are primarily used for showing a change in data over time. Bar graphs are used for making comparisons.

For example,

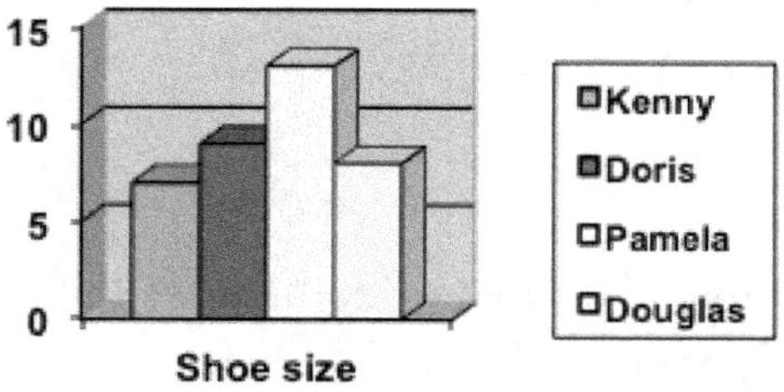

Bar graph

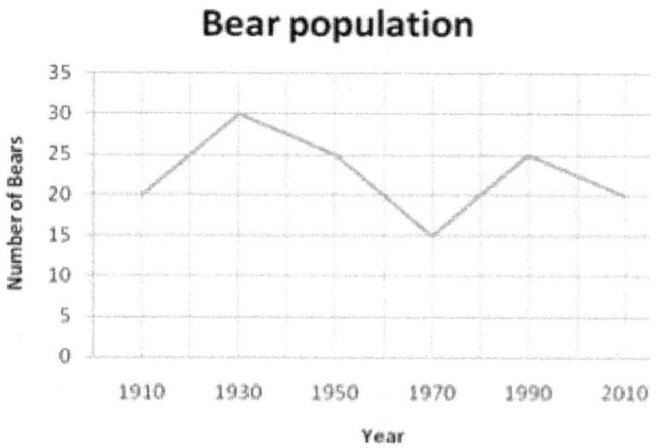

Line graph

Creating a Graph

When creating a graph, it is very important to make sure that the graph has a title and correct labels. The labels are the words that describe what is on the graph. In the bar graph above, the label is the shoe size. In the line graph above, the labels are the year and the weight.

The scale of the graph is also very important. The scales should be created so that the range (the difference between the highest and lowest numbers) and the distribution (the time frame) will accommodate all of the data.

For example, the data you have represents the height of trees over time. The height of the trees range from 3 meters to 76 meters and the time is over a period of 15 years.

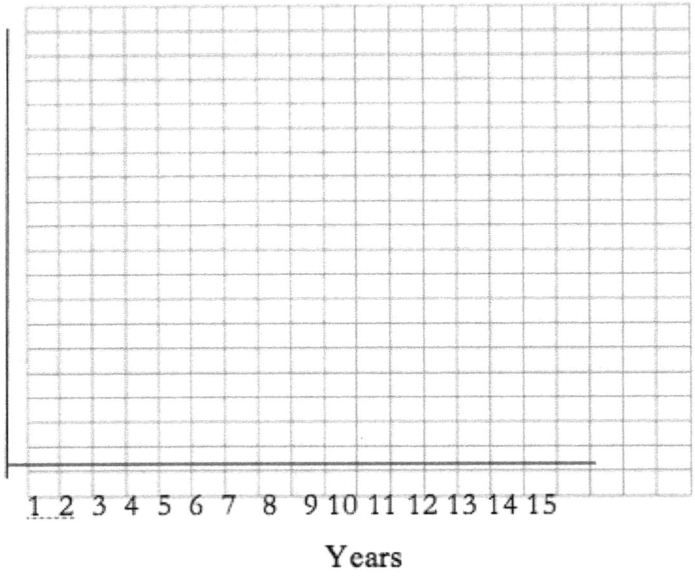

The graph has enough lines to put each year on a separate line. For the range, there are not enough lines for each meter to be listed separately, so you will need to figure out what scale to use.

Line Graphs

A line graph is a graph that uses points connected by lines to show how something changes in value. Often times, line graphs show data over a period of time.

Line graphs are often created using tables of data. The table below has data on the temperatures in a city.

Day	Temperature
1	43°
2	53°
3	50°
4	57°
5	59°
6	67°

The graph below them uses a line to show the increase in temperature over the six days.

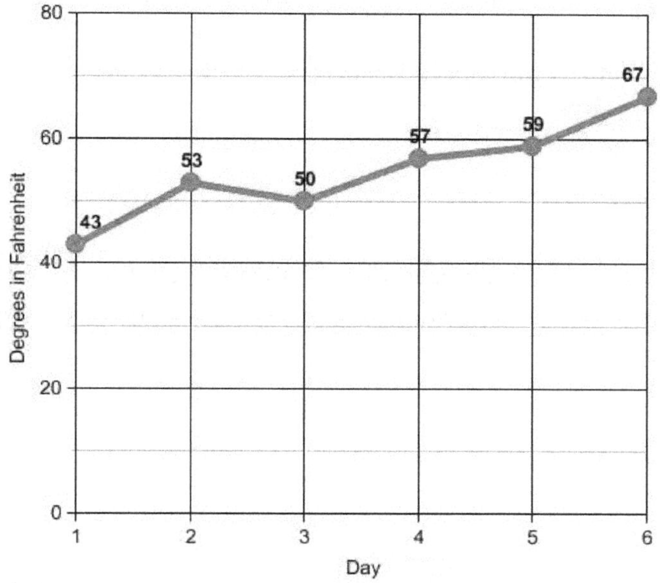

When creating a line graph, it is important to label the axis appropriately.

For the example above, the days are numbered by ones because only 6 days were measured. The degrees are numbered by tens because the highest temperature is 67.

Analyzing Data

There are several terms that are commonly used when analyzing data. Those terms are mean, median, mode and range.

The mean is the average of all of the numbers being analyzed. In order to find the mean, you must add up all of the numbers in a list or on a graph. Then, divide the total by how many numbers there are.

For example, the set of numbers is (3, 17, 4, 9, 11, 15)

Step 1: Add up all of the numbers: 3 + 17 + 4 + 9 + 11 + 15 = 59

Step 2: Count how many numbers are in the set. There are 6 numbers in the

set.

Step 3: Divide the total (59) by the numbers in the set (6) to get the mean.

59 ÷ 6 = 9.83

The median is the middle number in a list of numbers. In order to find the median, the numbers must be in numerical order from smallest to largest, so it is often necessary to rewrite your list of numbers.

For example, the set of numbers is (3, 17, 4, 9, 11, 15)

Step 1: Look to see if the numbers are in order from smallest to largest. If they are not, they must be rewritten: 3, 4, 9, 11, 15, 17

Step 2: Find the middle number. If the set contains an even number of numbers, find the two middle numbers. In this case, the two middle numbers are 9 and 11.

Step 3: This step is only necessary if there are two middle numbers! If there are, you must find the average of those two numbers. In this case, the average of 9 and 11 is 10.

The mode is the number that occurs most often. There can be no mode in a list of numbers if none of the numbers are repeated.

For example, the set of numbers is (3, 17, 4, 9, 11, 15). There is no mode in this set of numbers because none of the numbers are repeated.

The set of numbers is (4, 8, 2, 15, 8, 3, 2, 9, 8). There are several numbers that are repeated, the numbers 2 and 8. However, the mode is the number that occurs most often. 8 occurs three times and 2 occurs only twice. Therefore, the mode is 8.

The range is the difference between the largest and the smallest numbers. To find the range, you simply subtract the smallest number from the largest number.

For example, the set of numbers is (3, 17, 4, 9, 11, 15). To find the range, subtract the smallest number (3) from the largest number (17). 17 – 3 = 14. The range of this set of numbers is 14.

Exercises

Each of these terms is used to answer questions and provide more information about the data you are using.

Clinton is collecting data on the number of yellow leaves on the maple trees near his house. He has his information in a table.

Tree	Number of Yellow Leaves
1	34
2	16
3	28
4	32
5	18
6	34
7	24

1. What is the median for Clinton's data? ___________

2. What is the range for Clinton's data? ___________

3. What is the mode for Clinton's data? ___________

4. What is the mean for Clinton's data? ___________

5. Teddy counts the number of marbles in 8 different bags. (28, 33, 31, 28, 29, 34, 35, 28) What is the mode? ___________

6. Given the following set, what is the median? (129, 4, -8, 65, -19, 88, 74)

   ____

7. You collect data about the number of movies people have seen in the past month. You get the numbers 2, 0, 4, 1, 6, and 3. What is the median?

____

8. Karen collects data about the ages of people's pets. She get the numbers 5, 17, 13, 6, 2 and 9. What is the mean?

____

9. You collect data on the height of bean plants. You get the numbers 42, 46, 44, 40, 38 and 50. The height of your plant is the same as the median. What is it?

____

10. Create a line graph using the following table:

Week	Height of Sunflower
1	5 inches
2	12 inches
3	19 inches
4	23 inches
5	28 inches

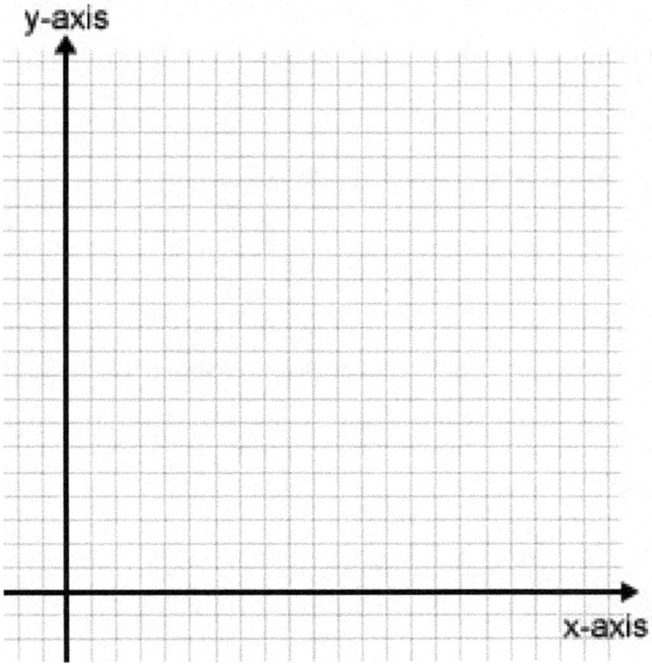

11. Stephen collects data about the pounds of food you eat in a week and get the numbers 17, 20, 23, 19, 16 and 13. If he plotted the line, what direction would it go?

____

12. Rebecca collects data on the number of pages you read in a day. She gets the numbers 13, 18, 24, 27, 23, 27 and 15. What is the range? __________

13. Should John use a survey or observation to collect data on how many nights families sit down and eat dinner together? __________

14. Hector likes to keep a record of how many times he hits a ball at batting practice. (15, 25, 39, 24, 11, 32, 27) What is the mean? __________

15. Mike practices his saxophone every day. He records the number of minutes he practices for 10 days. Mike wants to know the average number of minutes he practices every day so that he can tell his teacher. (34, 46, 21, 38, 36, 22, 19, 39, 36, 24)

____

16. Given the following set, what is the mode? (6, 29, 41, 14, 24, 8, 11)

____

17. Raphael knows how tall seven of his friends are in inches. (60, 64, 69, 62, 66, 59, 61) What is the average height of his friends? __________

18. Given the following set, what is the range? (7, 21, 49, 54, 13, 33, 4)

____

19. Carla babysits after school. She keeps track of the money that she makes each day so that she can figure out the average amount of money she makes per day. (14, 25, 18, 21, 33) __________

20. Sam notices his tomato plants are growing at different rates. What is the best way for Sam to figure out how tall his plants are?
    a. Measure
    b. Observation
    c. Survey

Quiz

Daphne is collecting data on the time it takes for her to do homework each night. She has her information in a table.

Night	Time to do Homework
1	22 minutes
2	27 minutes
3	35 minutes
4	27 minutes
5	22 minutes
6	27 minutes
7	16 minutes

1. What is the median for Daphne's data? ______________

2. What is the range for Daphne's data? ______________

3. What is the mode for Daphne's data? ______________

4. What is the mean for Daphne's data? ______________

5. Should Alyssa use measurement or observation to find the length of driveways in her neighborhood? ______________

6. Tracy keeps track of the number of birds who eat at her bird feeder every day for a week. (4, 12, 6, 8, 4, 7, 9) What is the average number of birds who eat at her bird feeder?
   ____

7. Crista loves to run. She keeps track of how many miles she runs over five days. (15, 8, 9, 12, 7) What is the range? ______________

8. Given the following set of data, what is the mode? (7, 12, 6, 12, 9, 5, 8, 5)

____

9. Eddie reads every night before he goes to bed and keeps track of the number of pages he reads. (34, 29, 12, 18, 25) What is the median?________________

10. Create a graph using the following table:

Day	Minutes Practiced the Violin
1	25 minutes
2	20 minutes
3	30 minutes
4	35 minutes
5	40 minutes
6	35 minutes

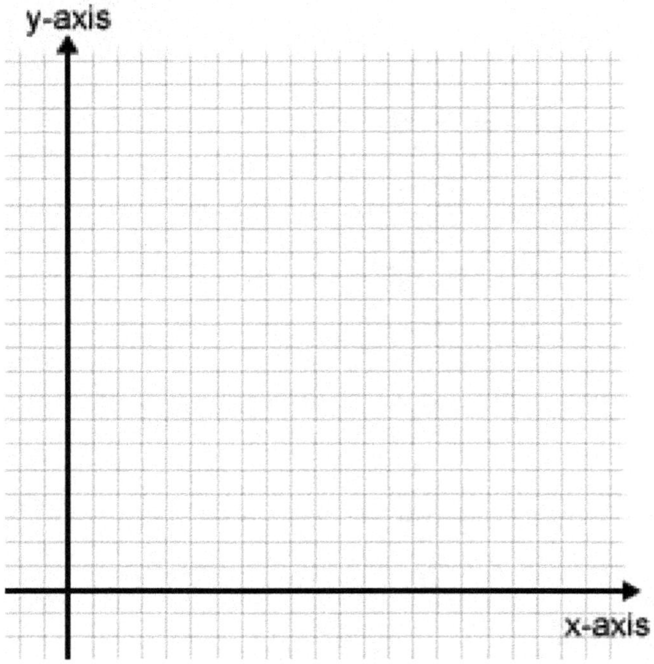

Decimals

Decimals are numbers that are less than one. You can also think about decimals as parts of a whole. Decimals can be combined with whole numbers so that you have a whole and a part. For example, you can have 2 wholes and a half, which would be 2.5. In this case, the decimal has two parts, the integer part and the fractional part. The integer part of the decimal is the whole number. The fractional part is the part of the whole.

For example in 2.5, 2 is the integer part and .5 is the fractional part

The parts of the whole, the decimal, are represented in the base ten system using a decimal point. When looking at a decimal, it is important to remember that the farther away (to the right) from the decimal point the number is, the smaller it is.

For example, 3.402 is smaller than 3.04 because .402 is a smaller piece than .04 is. .402 represents four hundred and two thousandths and .04 represents four hundredths. Four hundred two thousandths is smaller than four hundredths.

Decimals can also be thought of as fractions. The decimal 2.5 can also be thought of as 2 ½. Thinking of a decimal as a fraction may make it easier to think of the decimal as a part of a whole.

For example, the decimal .482 is four hundred eighty two thousandths. This could also be written as a fraction and would be 482/1000.

Whole numbers and decimals are easily identified because of place value. Place value allows us to figure out how many ones, tens, hundreds, etc. there are in each number.

Place Value

When looking at numbers, it is easy to figure out big or small they are because of place value. Place value is the position of a digit in a number and its value. Place value helps us to understand a numbers relationship to the other numbers as well as to be able to identify very large or very small numbers.

Place value is a system of representation in which the position of a number with respect to a point determines its value. When you move right away from the decimal point, each position gets ten times bigger. When you move left away from the decimal point, each position gets ten times smaller. Every place that the number is put in has a name. Those names are then used when identifying a number.

For example, the number 35.82 is read as thirty five and eighty-two hundredths

The decimal point is the most important part of the number. Without the decimal, you would not know what the value of each place is. Decimal points are in every number, including whole numbers.

For example, the number 67 can also be written as 67.0. You do not need to say and zero tenths, but having the decimal point in the number allows you to identify each of the places correctly.

The example below shows a very large number. Knowing place value will help you to identify the value of each digit. Place value will also be incredibly helpful when comparing or ordering numbers.

4	8	2	3	8	1	8	2	0	2	4	7	.	5	3	6
Hundred Billions	Ten Billions	Billions	Hundred Millions	Ten Millions	Millions	Hundred thousands	Ten thousands	Thousands	Hundreds	Tens	Ones	Decimal Point	Tenths	Hundredths	Thousandths

The value of the digits are what allow you to identify the number as a whole rather than as individual numbers. In the base ten system, the value of the digits is based on the number ten.

Base Ten

The decimal numbering system that is most commonly used is a base ten system. The base ten system means that there are only ten symbols to use when representing numbers. Those ten symbols are 0, 1, 2, 3, 4, 5, 6, 7, 8, 9. After those numbers have been used, we add a zero after the one and continue using each of the numbers in order.

For example, after 9, you put a 0 after the 1 and create 10, then a 1 after the 1 to create 11, etc. Once you get to 19, you run out again and so you put a zero after two and create 20.

Base ten blocks represent different values. They look like this:

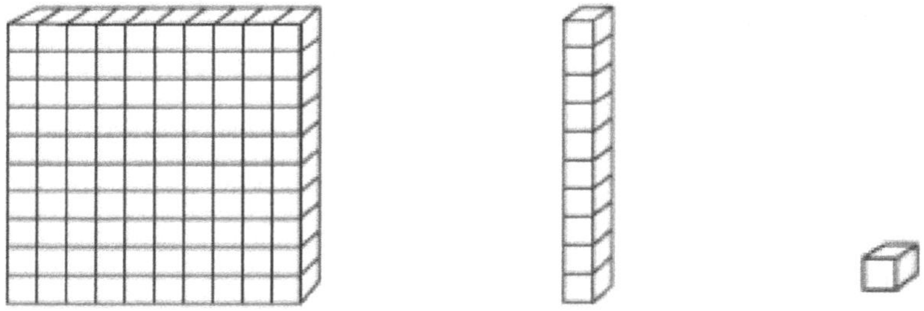

Each of the base ten blocks can represent a different value. For example, if the biggest block represents a tenth, the middle block would represent a hundredth and the smallest block would represent a thousandth.

When using base ten block, it is very important to know what value the block is representing in order to correctly answer the questions or correctly represent different values.

Ordering Numbers

Sometimes it is necessary to put numbers in numerical order, from ascending (smallest to largest) or descending (largest to smallest). Some of the reasons that numbers could be put in numerical order are shelving books at the library, house numbers on houses or pages in a book.

When ordering numbers, it is always important to start by looking at the largest place and working down. It does not matter if the largest number is in the millions or if the largest number is in the thousandths. Always start with the place all the way to the left.

Steps for ordering numbers in descending order:

Step 1: Identify the largest place.

Step 2: Compare the numbers based on the largest place. If the numbers are the same, look at the next place.

Step 3: Compare all of the numbers based on each place value.

Step 4: When the largest number has been identified, write that down and continue to write the numbers in descending order.

For example, 945,285 920,762 712,597 Look at the largest place. You can see that the first two numbers both have a 9. To compare these numbers, you need to look at the next place to the right to see if they are different. You see that in the next place over, the 4 is bigger than the 2, which makes 945,285 bigger than 920,762. You can see that 712,597 is the smallest number because in the first place that was compared, in this example the hundred thousand place, the 7 is smaller than the 9.

Hint: It is easier to compare numbers when they are lined up vertically with the decimal point in the same place. If there are empty places at the end, you can add a zero to make it very easy to visually compare the numbers.

34.87

3.90

821.23

Steps for ordering numbers in ascending order are very similar to the steps for ordering numbers in descending order. The only difference is that when ordering numbers in ascending order, you must find the smallest number and write that down first.

Comparing Numbers

Numbers are often compared to find out which is larger and which is smaller. Comparing numbers is very similar to ordering numbers. You will follow the same steps to determine which number is bigger or smaller.

The symbols that are used to compare numbers are:

< is the less than symbol

> is the greater than symbol

= is equal to

When using the "less than" symbol (<), the point always points toward the smaller number. When using the "greater than" symbol (>), the large, open part (that looks like a mouth) points toward the larger number. A good way to remember which way the symbol points is that the "mouth" always wants to eat the biggest number. The equal sign is only used when a number is exactly the same.

For example, numbers 63.8 and 63.80 are the same number. 63.80 has a zero at the end of it, but the zero has no value, so it does not change the number. An equal sign would be used when comparing 63.8 and 63.80.

Adding and Subtracting Decimals

Decimals can be added and subtracted just like whole numbers. When adding decimals, numbers can be carried just like when adding whole numbers. When subtracting decimals, numbers can be borrowed just like when subtracting whole numbers.

When adding or subtracting decimals, the most important step to remember is that the decimal points must be lined up. When you line up the decimal point, you ensure that the places are lined up with each other.

For example, 13.45 + 7.2 is the problem you are trying to solve. To solve it, line them up like this: 13.45

+ 7.2

You can even add a zero after the 2 to ensure the places are lined up correctly. You will then be able to add the hundredths place to the hundredths place, the tenths place to the tenths place and the ones place to the ones. The answer would be 20.65.

If the decimal points are not lined up, the answer will not be correct. If you were to line up the first numbers and not the decimal point, you would get 85.45 as an answer, which is not correct.

Always remember to line up the decimal point!

Exercises

1. Compare the two numbers: 63.08 6.308

2. Which number is larger? 456354.127 or 456354.129 ____________

3. What is the value of the number 5 in 3123.95? ____________

4. Add 43.8 and 127.02 ____________

5. Put the numbers in descending order: 542.8, 512.03, 542.4, 512.72

   ____

6. Compare the two numbers: 0.854 0.85

7. 129.45 - 94.031 = ____________

8. Which number is smaller? 4563.483 or 4563.783 ____________

9. Write the decimal .68 as a fraction ____________

10. What is the value of the number 9 in 934.082? ____________

11. 67.351 + 8.523 = ____________

12. Put the numbers is ascending order: 341.982, 341.985, 349.71, 346.012

    ____

13. Which number is larger? 512346.8 or 516346.8 ____________

14. Compare the two numbers: 2.010 2.010 ____________

15. 5.391 - .835 = ____________

16. Put the numbers in ascending order: 1.394, 2.8713, 1.492, 1.842

    ____

17. Which number is smaller? 78.916 or 78.956 ____________

18. Compare the two numbers: 0.11 0.111 ____________

19. Write the decimal .451 as a fraction ____________

20. 78.092 + 498.23 = ____________

Quiz

1. Compare the two numbers: 34.67 3.467

2. Which number is larger? 587.23 or 587.32 ____________

3. What is the value of the number 3 in 901.234? ____________

4. Add 219.08 and 76.341 ____________

5. Put the numbers in descending order: 98.342, 98.38, 97.423, 97.03

   ____

6. Compare the two numbers: 0.213 0.22

7. 56.7 – 52.82 = ____________

8. Which number is smaller? 4.623 or .4623 ____________

9. Write the decimal .741 as a fraction ____________

10. What is the value of the number 4 in 564.87? ____________

Fractions

Fractions are very important. A fraction is a part of a whole. Fractions are everywhere in daily life. When eating a pizza, cake or pie, or brownies, fractions are used. Any time that a whole is cut into pieces, those pieces are fractions. Look around and you can see fractions in all aspects of your life. Fractions can be found in quilts, when using a recipe or when using money.

When looking at a fraction, you can see that fractions have a numerator (the top number), which represents the number of parts of the whole there are and a denominator (the bottom number), which represents the total number of parts of the whole. Fractions are written with the numerator over the denominator. That is done by writing one number and then drawing a line under it and writing a number under the line.

For example, ½ or $\frac{1}{2}$

When working with fractions, the easiest way to understand the concept is to picture either a circle or a square. The denominator represents the parts of the whole. If the denominator is 8, picture the circle or square being cut into 8 pieces. The numerator represents the parts of the whole that are being used. Then, picture the pieces being used being colored in or taken away. Drawing the shapes, divide them into the number of pieces indicated by the denominator and then color in the number of pieces indicated by the numerator. Being able to visualize the parts of the whole will help when working with fractions.

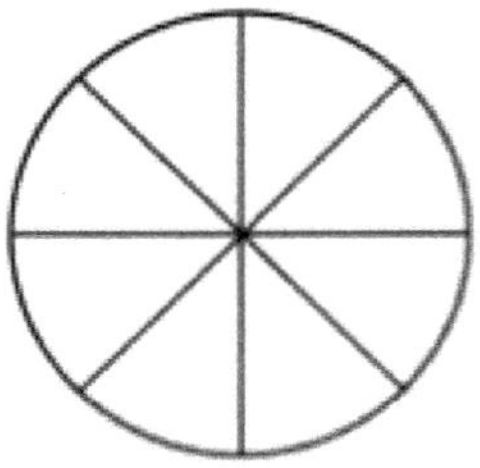 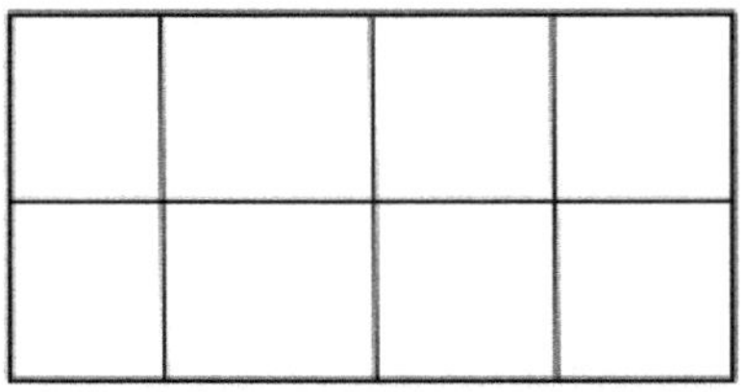

For example, in the fraction 5/8, the picture that you could draw would look like this:

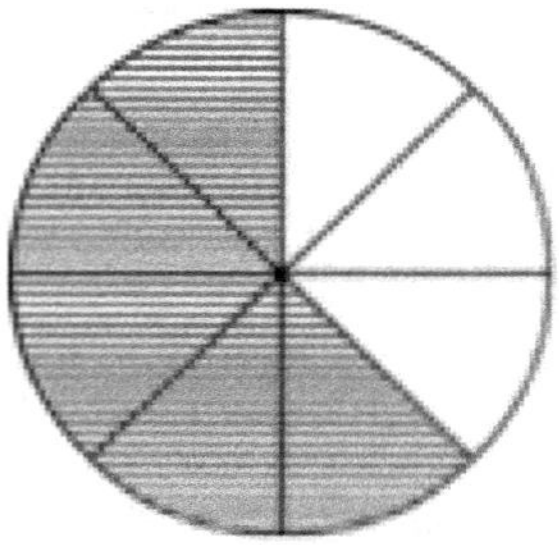

Seeing the fraction makes it much easier to then understand what 5/8 means and to work with that fraction.

Usually, the numerator in fractions is smaller than the denominator. When the numerator is smaller, it means that there are less pieces than there are whole parts. For example, in the fraction 2/6, the whole is split into six pieces. There are only two of those six pieces.

When the numerator is larger, it means that there are more pieces than there are whole parts. For example, in the fraction 8/6, the whole is split into six pieces. There are eight pieces, which is more than one whole.

There are several different types of fractions. There are regular fractions where the numerator is smaller than the denominator. There are improper fractions where the numerator is bigger than the denominator. There are mixed fractions that consist of both a whole number and a regular fraction.

Improper Fractions

Fractions that have a numerator that is bigger than the denominator are called improper fractions.

For example, $^{12}/_{4}$ or $^{16}/_{6}$

Improper fractions can be left with the numerator bigger than the denominator, or they can be changed or reduced to mixed or whole numbers. Whether or not an improper fraction is left with a bigger numerator than denominator or whether it is changed or reduced to a mixed or whole number, the value of the fraction does not change.

To change or reduce an improper fraction to either a mixed or a whole number, you will divide the numerator by the denominator. Using $^{12}/_{4}$ as an example, you can see that it will divide evenly, leaving you with a whole number.

For example, $12 \div 4 = 3$

For improper fractions that are not evenly divided, such as $^{16}/_{6}$, you need to figure out how many whole numbers are in that fraction. You will then use the remainder as the numerator for the fractional piece of the mixed number.

For example, $16 \div 6 = 2$ remainder $4 = 2\ ^{4}/_{6}$ You could then reduce $2\ ^{4}/_{6}$ down even further by dividing both the numerator and the denominator by 2. That would leave you with an answer of $2\ ^{2}/_{3}$.

Equivalent Fractions

Equivalent fractions are fractions that are equal. Equivalent fractions can look exactly the same, but they can also look different. For example, $^{2}/_{3}$ and $^{4}/_{6}$ are equivalent, but look different. If the fractions do not look exactly the same, it is necessary to figure out if the fraction is equivalent. To do that, will multiply or divide both the numerator and the denominator by the same number. In the case of $^{2}/_{3}$ and $^{4}/_{6}$, both the numerator and the denominator in $^4/_6$ is divided by 2. That leaves $^2/_3$ and allows you to see that $^2/_3$ and $^4/_6$ are equal.

Another example is 3/6 and ½. 3/6 cannot be divided by 2 because 2 is not divisible by 2. Therefore, to find out if the fractions are equivalent, ½ must be multiplied by the number that will make it have the same denominator as 3/6. That means it must be multiplied by 3. When both the numerator and the denominator are multiplied by 3, the fraction is 3/6. 3/6 is equivalent to 3/6.

Adding and Subtracting Fractions

Fractions can be added and subtracted. Fractions that have the same denominator can easily be added or subtracted. In that case, the only part of the fraction that is added or subtracted is the numerator.

For example, 3/5 + 2/5. The denominator in both fractions is 5. To solve the addition problem, add 3 + 2 to get 5. That numerator is then put over the denominator for an answer of 5/5.

An example of a subtraction problem is 7/9 – 5/9. The denominator in both fractions is 9. To solve the subtraction problem, subtract 7 – 5 to get 2. That numerator is then put over the denominator for an answer of 2/9.

If the fractions do not have the same denominator additional steps are needed.

Step 1: Identify the denominators

Step 2: Identify the greatest common factor

Step 3: Identify the number that the denominator needs to be multiplied by to get the greatest common factor

Step 4: Multiply both the numerator and the denominator by that number

For example, 4/5 and 2/3 can be given the same denominator. 5 and 3 are the denominators. The greatest common factor of 5 and 3 is 15. To make 4/5 have a denominator of 15, it must be multiplied by 3. To make 2/3 have a denominator of 15, it must be multiplied by 5.

Multiply both the numerator and the denominator in 4/5 by 3. That makes the fraction into 12/15. Multiply both the numerator and the denominator in 2/3 by 5. That makes the fraction 10/15.

The addition problem 4/5 + 2/3 can be solved once the denominators were made to be the same number. The problem would be rewritten as 12/15 + 10/15. The problem could then be solved easily. The answer would be 22/15.

Multiplying and Dividing Fractions

Fractions can also be multiplied and divided just like they can be added and subtracted. Unlike with adding or subtracting fractions, both the numerator and the denominator are involved in multiplication and division.

When multiplying fractions, the denominators of each of the fractions can be different. Multiplying fractions is very easy. You simply multiply the numerators together and then multiply the denominators together. The numbers in the answer that you get may be big. In that case, reducing the fraction may be necessary.

Step 1: Multiply the numerators

Step 2: Multiply the denominators

Step 3: Write the fraction with the numerator answer over the denominator answer

Step 4: Check to see if the answer can be reduced at all. If it can be, reduce the fraction to the lowest terms.

For example, 5/9 × 6/7 First start by multiplying the numerators. 5 × 6 = 30. Then, multiply the denominators. 9 × 7= 63. Write the new fraction as 30/63. The fraction can be reduced. 3 is the least common multiple. Divide both 30 and 63 by 3 to get 10/21.

When dividing fractions, both the numerator and the denominator are used. Dividing fractions is similar to multiplying fractions. The main difference is that the reciprocal of the second fraction needs to be found.

The reciprocal is a number divided by 1. In terms of fractions, the reciprocal is the number turned upside down. The numerator becomes the denominator and the denominator becomes the numerator. For example, the reciprocal of ¾ is 4/3.

The steps for diving fractions are:

Step 1: Find the reciprocal of the second fraction

Step 2: Multiply the numerators

Step 3: Multiply the denominators

Step 4: Write the fraction with the numerator answer over the denominator answer

Step 5: Check to see if the answer can be reduced at all. If it can be, reduce the fraction to the lowest terms.

For example, 5/8 ÷ 3/5 The first step is to find the reciprocal of the second fraction, which is 3/5. The reciprocal is 5/3. Next, multiply the numerators which are now 5 and 5. 5 × 5= 25. Then, multiply the denominators. The denominators are now 8 and 3. 8 × 3 = 24. Write the fraction with the numerator over the denominator. The answer is 25/24. That fraction can be reduced to become a mixed number. The mixed number would be 1 1/25.

Exercises

1. Which fraction is equivalent to $^{5}/_{7}$? $^{5}/_{14}$ $^{10}/_{14}$ $^{10}/_{12}$
2. Reduce $^{23}/_{3}$ __________
3. Which fraction is larger? $^{3}/_{5}$ or $^{4}/_{10}$ __________
4. $^{5}/_{8} + ^{3}/_{8} =$ __________
5. Find a fraction that is equivalent to 1 ¾ __________
6. $½ \times ^{13}/_{7} =$ __________
7. Reduce $^{19}/_{5}$ __________
8. $^{4}/_{5} - ^{3}/_{10} =$ __________
9. Which fraction is equivalent to $^{5}/_{9}$? $^{6}/_{18}$ $^{10}/_{18}$ $^{10}/_{20}$
10. $^{22}/_{7} \div ^{3}/_{2} =$ __________
11. Find a fraction that is equivalent to $^{6}/_{7}$. __________
12. $^{12}/_{13} - ^{5}/_{13} =$ __________
13. $^{9}/_{14} \times ½ =$ __________
14. Reduce $^{17}/_{4}$ __________
15. Which fraction is larger? $^{3}/_{5}$ or $^{4}/_{10}$
16. $^{15}/_{20} + ^{4}/_{10} =$ __________
17. $^{8}/_{10} \div ^{6}/_{5} =$ __________
18. Find a fraction that is equivalent to 4 $^{7}/_{9}$ __________
19. $^{14}/_{22} + ^{16}/_{22} =$ __________
20. Reduce $^{50}/_{8}$ __________

Quiz

1. Which fraction is equivalent to $^{9}/_{15}$? $^{18}/_{30}$ $^{15}/_{22}$ $^{18}/_{20}$

2. Reduce $^{21}/_{4}$ __________

3. Which fraction is larger? $^{3}/_{6}$ or $^{7}/_{12}$ __________

4. $^{6}/_{12} + {}^{5}/_{6} =$ __________

5. Find a fraction that is equivalent to $2\,^{3}/_{5}$ __________

6. $^{15}/_{4} \times {}^{2}/_{9} =$ __________

7. Reduce $^{29}/_{6}$ __________

8. $^{5}/_{9} - {}^{2}/_{18} =$ __________

9. Which fraction is equivalent to $^{6}/_{18}$? $^{7}/_{9}$ $^{2}/_{6}$ $^{3}/_{6}$

10. $^{10}/_{12} \div {}^{4}/_{9} =$ __________

Geometry

Geometry is a part of math that involves points, lines and shapes. There are many different types of points, lines and shapes. These geometric objects are used in everyday life as well as in special professions.

Lines

There are many types of lines that exist in geometric shapes. Two of those types of lines are parallel and perpendicular lines. Parallel lines are lines that run next to each other and never touch. They will go on forever without touching.

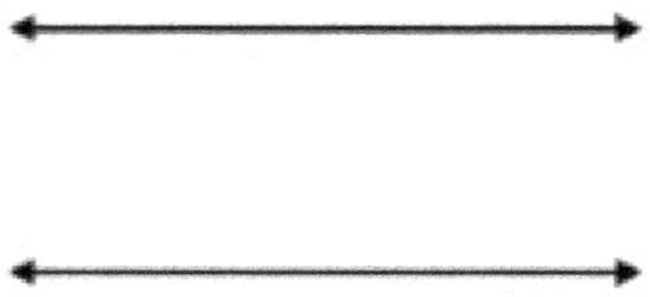

Perpendicular lines are lines that meet to form right angles. Perpendicular lines will only intersect one time and will always form right angles.

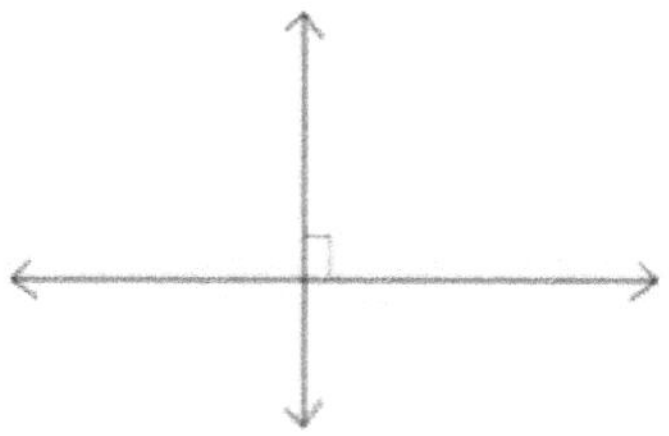

Lines can also be used to create other angles and shapes.

Angles

An angle is the space between two intersecting lines and often looks like the two lines come together to form what looks like the letter "V." Athletes, engineers, architects, carpenters, artists and many other professionals, use angles. There are many different types of angles and it is important to be able to tell the difference between them.

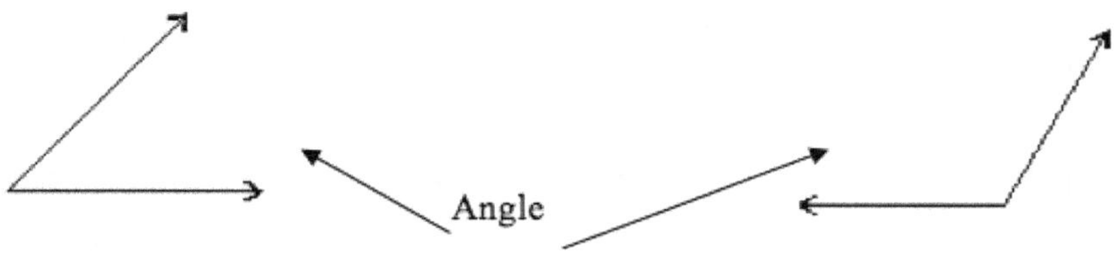

There are three different types of angles. Each of these angles is formed by intersecting lines. Angles get their name by the size of the angle that is formed.

Acute angles are angles that have a measurement of less than 90°.

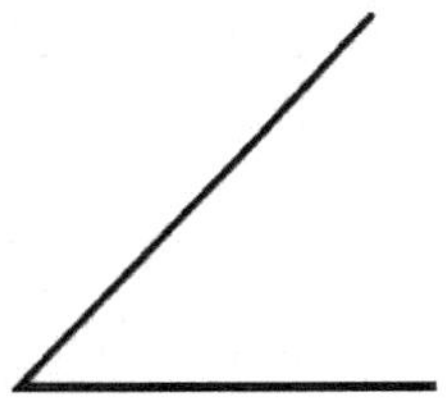

Right angles are angles that have a measurement of exactly 90°. Right angles are often formed by perpendicular lines.

Obtuse angles are angles that have a measurement of between 90° and 180°.

Straight angles are angles that have a measurement of exactly 180°.

Measuring an Angle

An angle is the space between two intersecting lines. All angles can be measured by using a protractor. The protractor can both help to measure angles and also help to draw them.

The measurement of an angle is the space between the two lines. Measuring an angle is done using a special tool called a protractor.

A protractor looks like this:

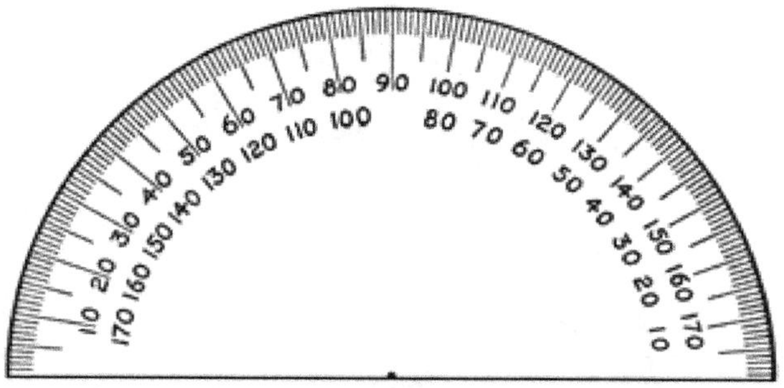

Protractors have two sets of numbers going in opposite directions. Those numbers are used to measure both acute and obtuse numbers. The dot or crossbow (+) at the bottom of the protractor should be lined up where the two lines meet. The bottom of the protractor should be lined up with one of the angle's lines.

This is what a protractor looks like measuring 10°.

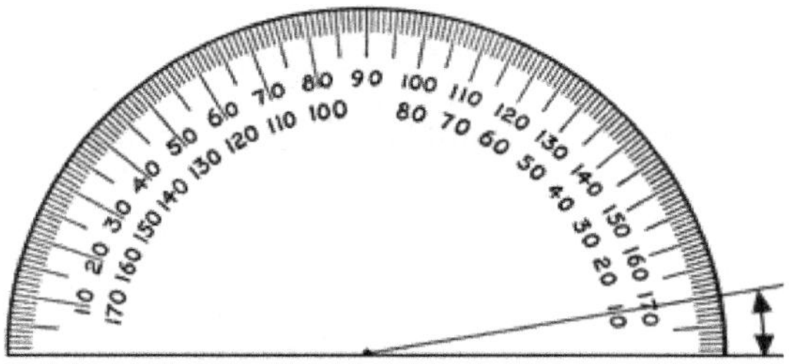

Drawing an Angle

Protractors are also used to draw angles. To draw an angle, start by drawing a straight line using the bottom of the protractor as a guide. Then put the small hole or dot at the bottom of the protractor at the end of the line. Find the number of the angle you are trying to draw and make a small mark above or below it. Then draw use the straight edge of the protractor to draw a line that connects the original line to the mark.

For example,

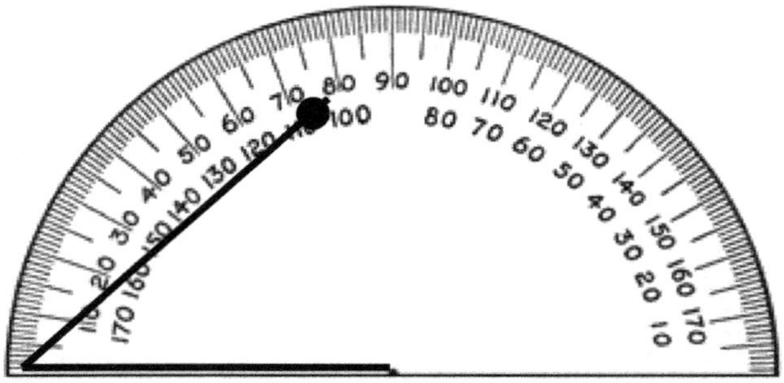

Triangles

There are many different types of triangles. All triangles have three sides and three angles that add up to be 180°. All triangles get their names based on the angles that they have as well as how the angles and sides exist in the triangle.

There are six different types of triangles that are the most common triangles. Those triangles are acute, right, obtuse, scalene, isosceles, and equilateral. Acute, right and obtuse triangles are named based on the types of angles that they have. Scalene, isosceles and equilateral triangles are based on the number of sides or angles that are equal.

An acute triangle is a triangle whose three angles are all acute angles, meaning that they are all less than 90°. For example,

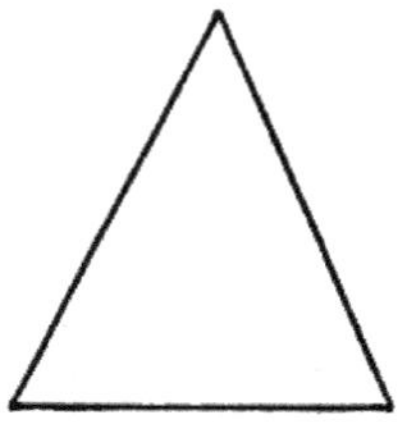

A right triangle is a triangle that has one angle equal to 90°. The other two angles are less than 90°. For example,

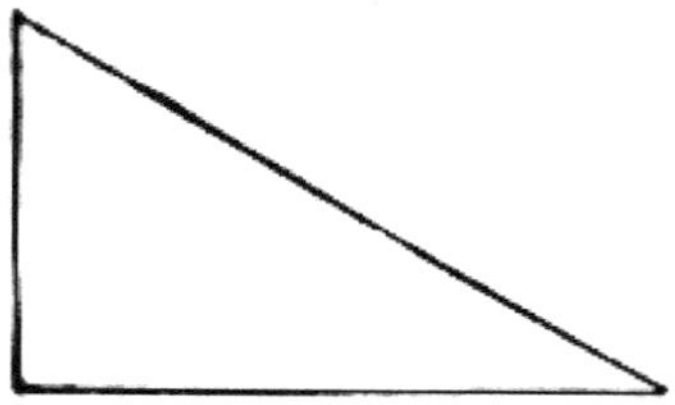

An obtuse triangle is a triangle that has one angle that is obtuse, meaning that it is between 90° and 180°. The other two angles are less than 90°. For example,

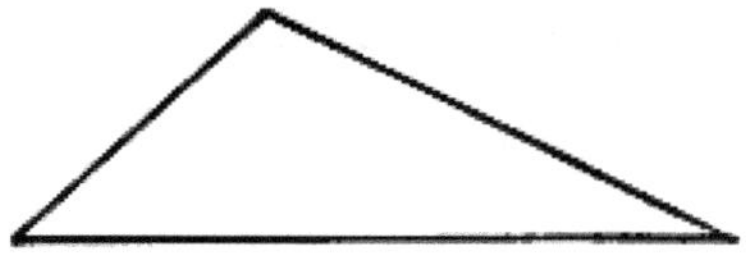

A scalene triangle has no sides or angles that are equal. For example,

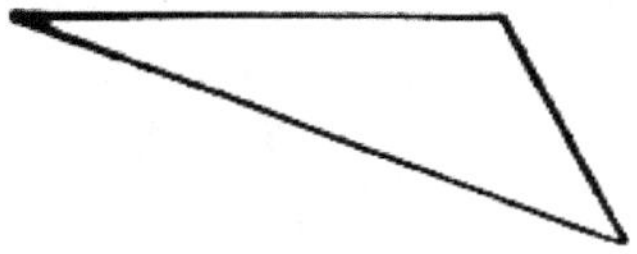

An isosceles triangle has two sides that are equal and two angles that are equal. For example,

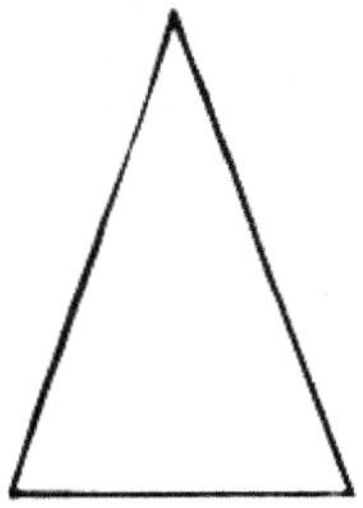

An equilateral triangle has all three sides and all three angles equal. The measure of each of the angles in an equilateral triangle is always 60°. For example,

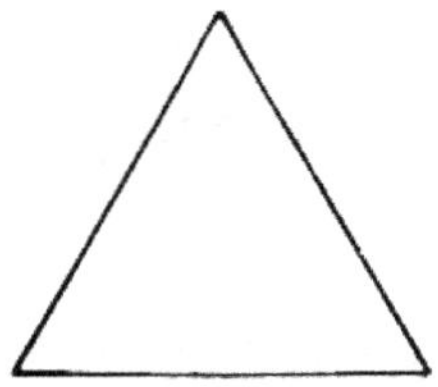

Determining the Type of Triangle

Triangles are named based on the measure of their sides and angles. It make it easy to identify those triangles, the sides and angles are generally marked if they are equal. Sides that are equal are usually marked with a little line cutting across the side. Angles that are equal are usually marked with an arc in the corner of the angle. Always look at the sides and angles of a triangle to see if they are marked. That will make it much easier to identify the type of triangle.

For example, two sides of the triangle below are equal so they are each marked with a line and the equal angles are marked with little arcs.

In looking at this triangle, the marks indicate that there are two equal sides and two equal angles. Those marks make it easy to identify this triangle as isosceles.

Dimensions

Geometric shapes can be either two-dimensional or three-dimensional. Two-dimensional shapes are shapes that look flat. They only have height and width or length. Three-dimensional shapes are shapes that look like you can reach out and touch them. They have height, width or length and depth.

Shapes

Everywhere you look you see shapes. Any shape that has at least three all straight lines are called polygons. There are some shapes that have less than 3 sides such as circles or hearts. Those shapes are not polygons. You also see two-dimensional shapes when you look at signs, read books or look at a map. It is important to be able to identify the objects that you are seeing.

Two-Dimensional Shapes

A two-dimensional shape is a shape that is flat (has only height and width or length) and has a line or lines that connect.

For example,

 or  or 

Polygons

A polygon is a two dimensional shape that is made from straight lines and all of the lines connect. Polygons have at least 3 sides and the sides do not cross each other. A regular polygon is a polygon that has all sides the same length and all angles are equal.

For example,

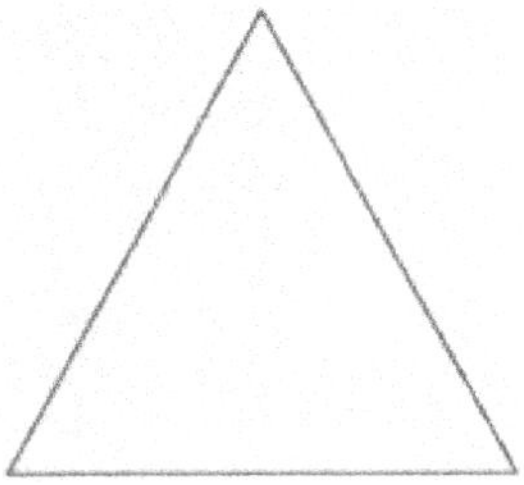 or 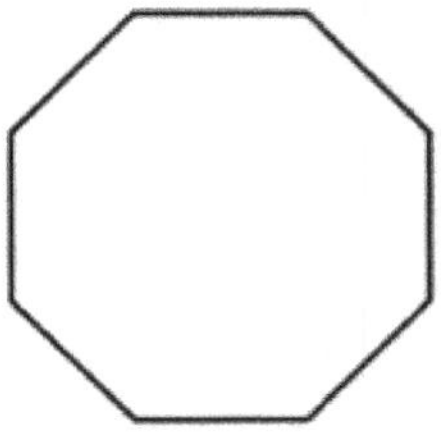

An irregular polygon is a polygon whose sides are not all the same length and whose angels are not equal.

For example,

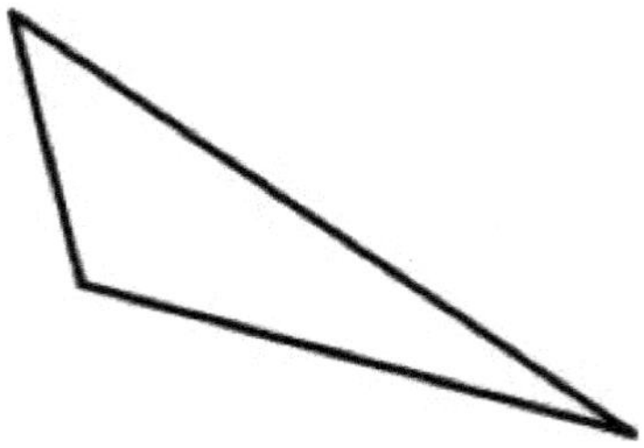

or

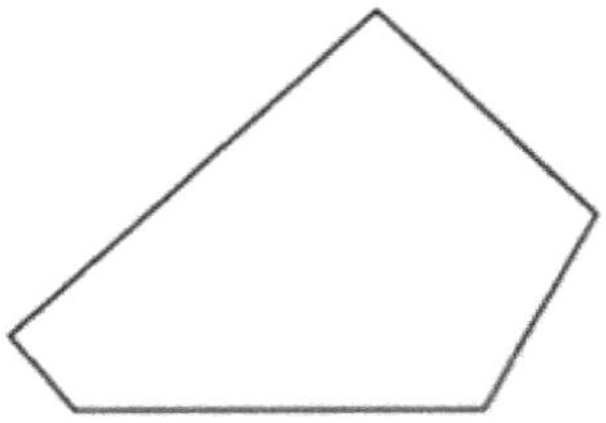

Prisms

A prism is another name for a three-dimensional shape. Three-dimensional shapes have height, width and depth and it looks like you can reach out and pick them up. Three-dimensional shapes are everywhere! There are some three-dimensional shapes that have specific names and it is important to know those. It is also important to be able to identify what is a prism and what is not.

A prism is a polyhedron, which means that it is a three-dimensional shape with flat faces and straight edges. Prisms have bases, which are polygons. Prisms are named by the shape of their bases.

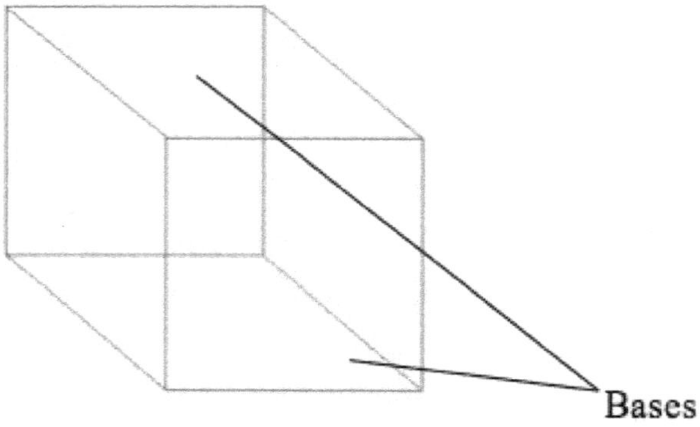

Right prisms are prisms that have bases that are parallel to each other. The angle between the base and the face is 90° and the bases are squares or rectangles

For example,

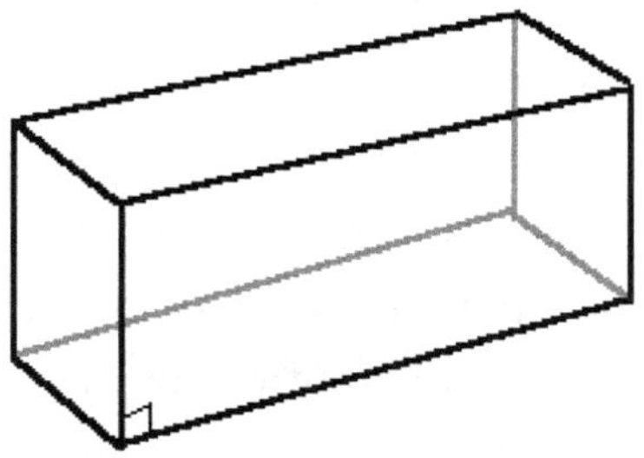

A pyramid is another type of prism. Pyramids are formed with one base and sides that meet at a point, also known as an apex. Pyramids are named by the shape of their base.

For example,

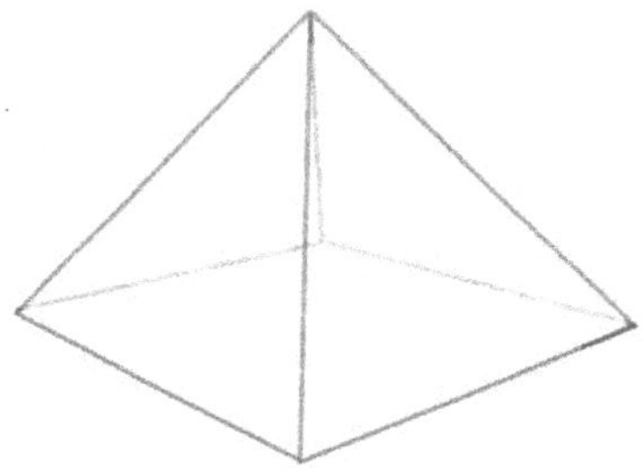

Other three-dimensional shapes are cones and cylinders.

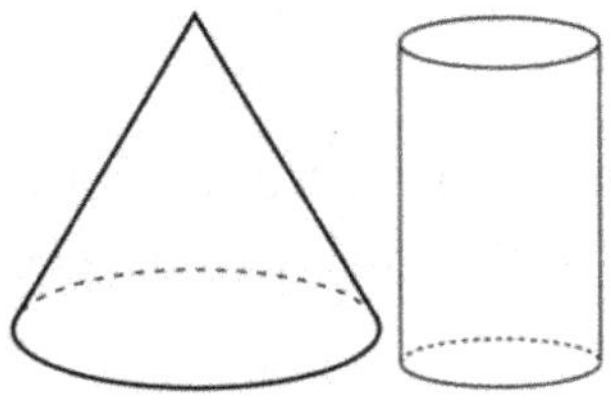

Critical Attributes

A critical attribute is something that a geometric shape MUST have. In geometry, different shapes have attributes that define them. Critical attributes are used when identifying shapes. If the critical attributes of a shape are unknown, it is almost impossible to identify that shape.

For example, squares have four equal sides. If there were a shape that had three equal sides or four sides that were not equal, it would not be a square.

Another example, equilateral triangles have three equal sides and three equal angles that are each 60°. When given that information, it would be easy to identify the triangle as equilateral. A triangle that did not have three equal sides or three equal angles would not be an equilateral triangle.

Congruency

Congruency is when shapes are the exact same size, shape and color. When figuring out if shapes are congruent, it may be necessary to flip, rotate or slide a shape. Shapes can be moved, but their size cannot be changed.

For example,

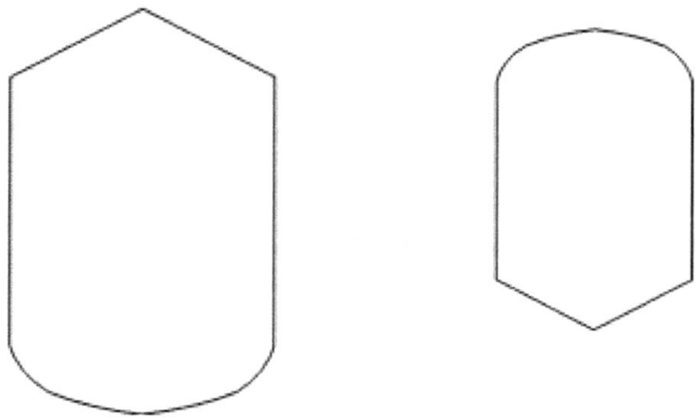

These shapes are the same shape. The shape on the right can be turned over to look like the shape on the left. However, they are not the same size so they will never be congruent.

Another example,

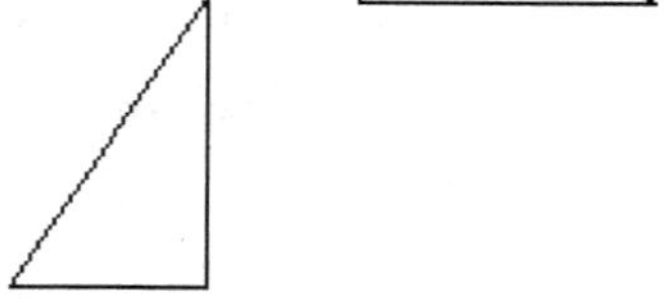

These triangles are the same size and shape. The triangle on the right can be flipped over to face the same direction as the triangle on the left. Because the triangles are the exact same size and shape, they are congruent.

Exercises

1. What is the measure of the angle? ____________

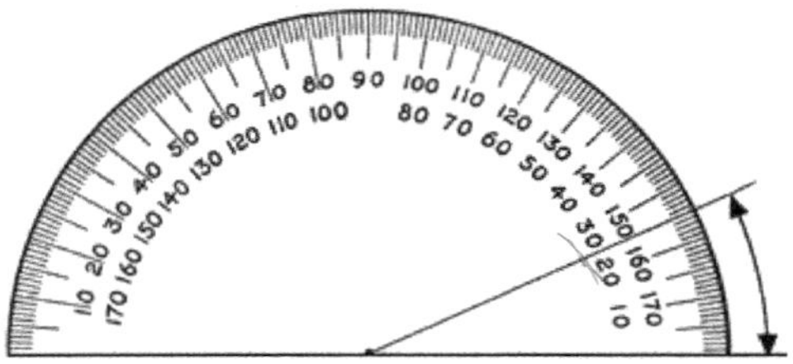

2. What type of angle is this?  ____________

3. What type of angle is exactly 90°? ____________

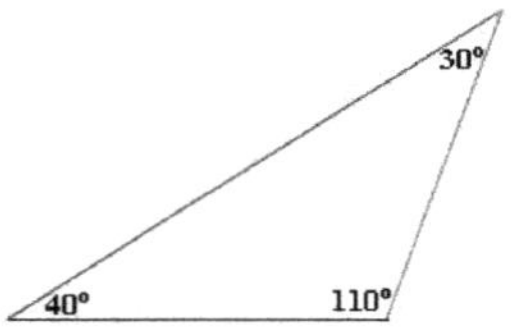

4. What type of triangle is this? ____________

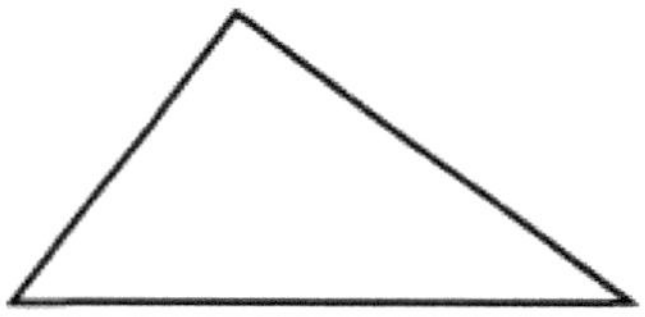

5. Is this triangle scalene or isosceles? ____________

6. An equilateral triangle has __________ equal sides and __________ equal angles.

7. What type of triangle is this? ____________

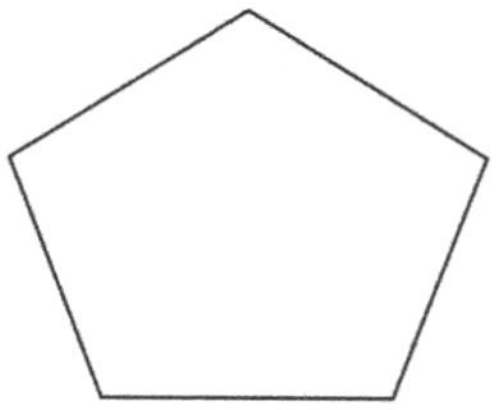

8. What are the critical attributes of this pentagon? ____________

9. Which prism is a right prism? 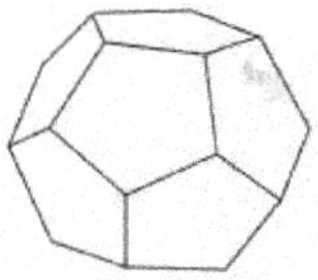 or 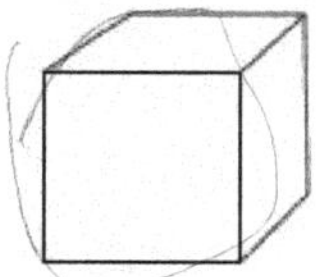

10. What type of pyramid is this? 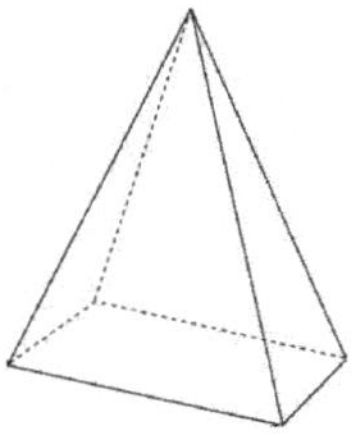 ______________

11. Which shape has parallel lines and acute angles? 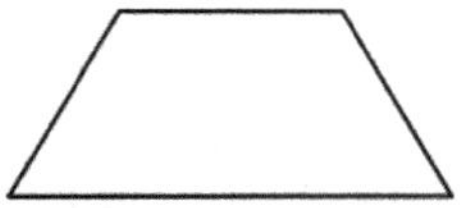 or 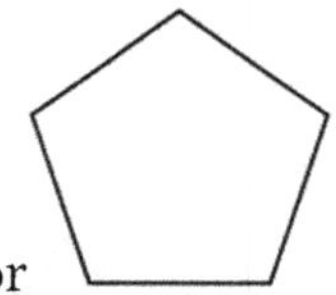

12. Which shape is two-dimensional? 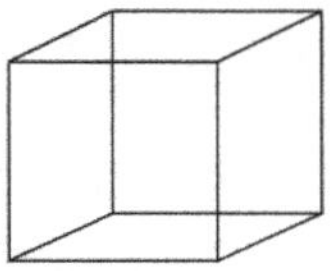 or 

13. What type of triangle is this? 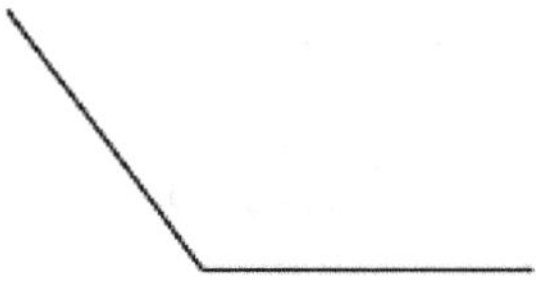 ______________

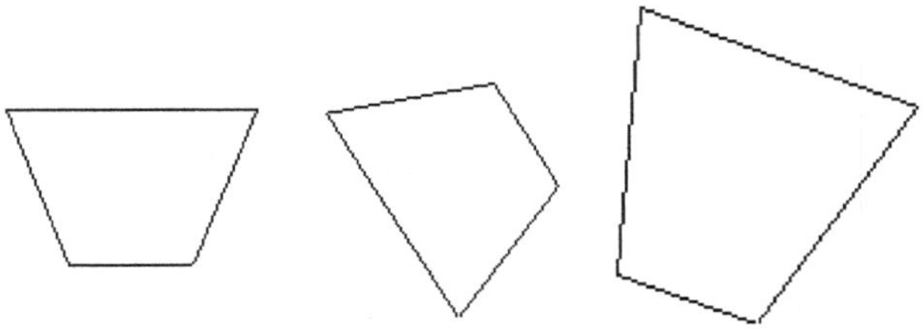

14. Which shapes are congruent?

15. Which shape has three sides, two equal sides and two equal angles? __________

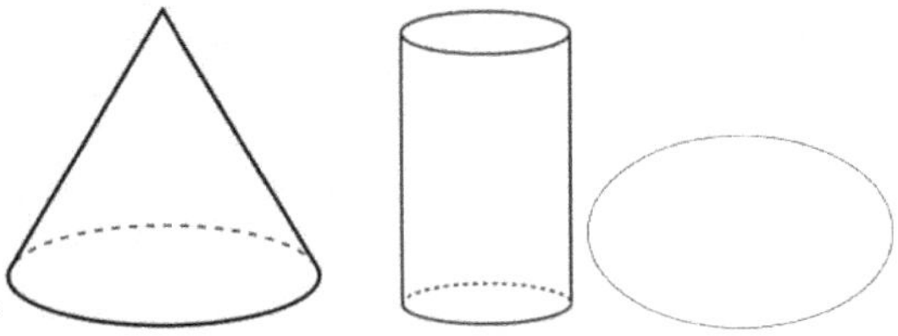

16. Which is not three-dimensional?

17. What are the measures of the angles in an equilateral triangle? ____________

18. Congruent shapes are ____

19. Which shape does not have a right angle?

20. An angle that has less than 90° is a __________________ angle.

Quiz

1. What is the measure of the angle? ______________

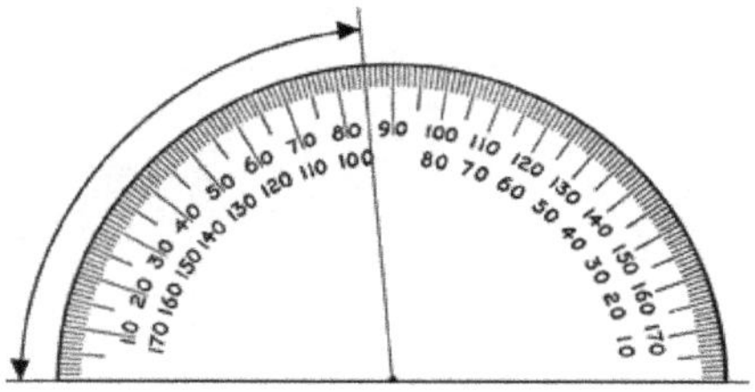

2. What type of angle is this? 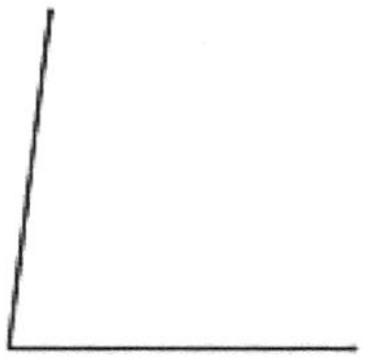 ______________

3. What type of angle is exactly 180°? ______________

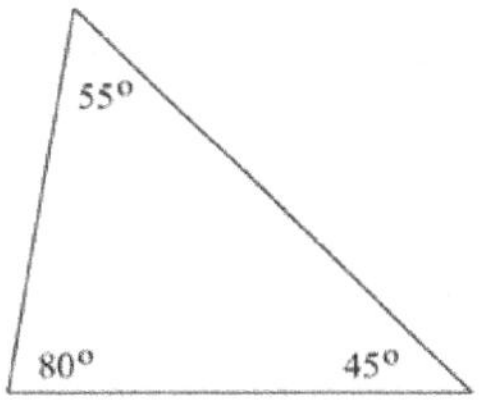

4. What type of triangle is this? ______________

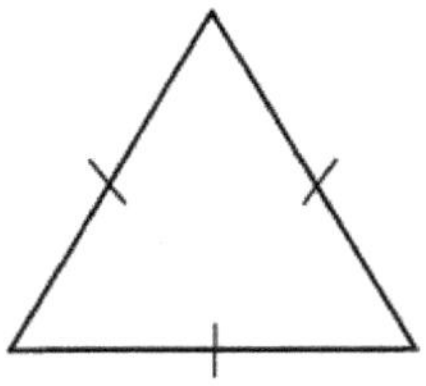

5. Is this triangle scalene or equilateral? ______________

6. An isosceles triangle has __________ equal sides and __________ equal angles.

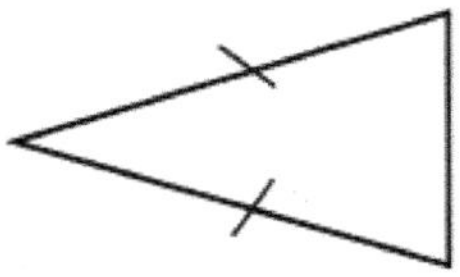

7. What type of triangle is this? ______________

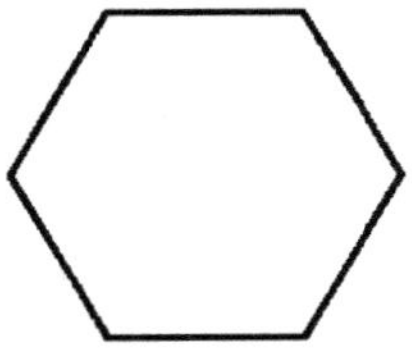

8. What are the critical attributes of this hexagon? ______________

9. Which prism is a hexagonal pyramid? 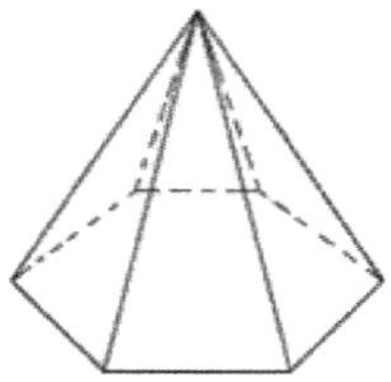 or 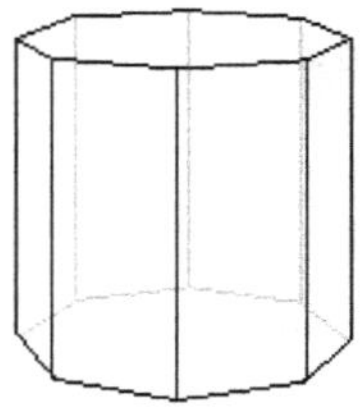

10. Which shape is not three-dimensional? 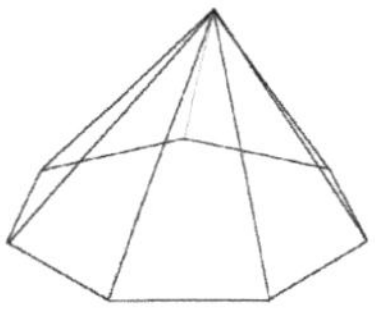 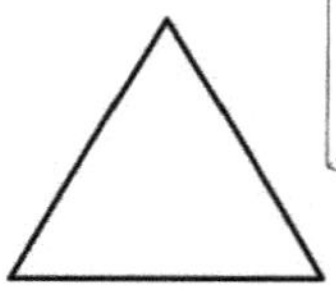 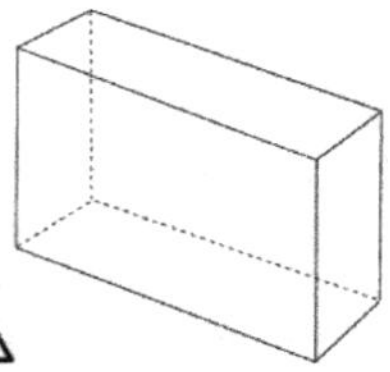

Measurement

Measurement is finding a number that shows the size or amount of something. There are times when it is necessary to measure an object and it is important to use the correct unit of measure. It would not make sense to use a huge unit of measure to measure a paper clip. It would also not make sense to use a tiny unit of measure to measure the length of a football field. Choosing the appropriate unit of measure is an important part of measuring.

Units of Measure

A unit of measure is the type of measurement that is used. There are different units of measure that are used for length, height, width and distance. The most commonly used units of measure are millimeter, centimeter, decimeter, meter, and kilometer.

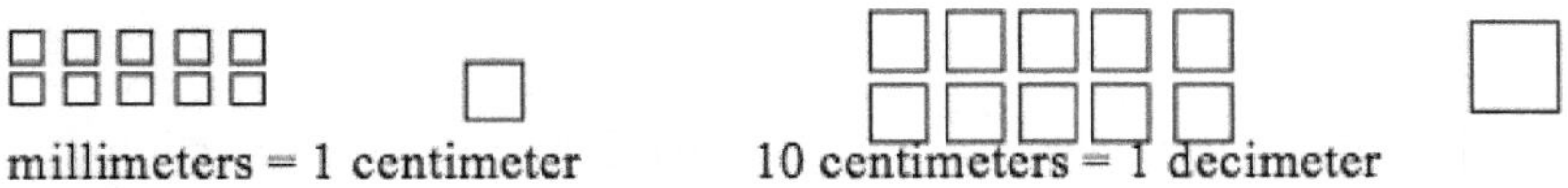

10 millimeters = 1 centimeter   10 centimeters = 1 decimeter

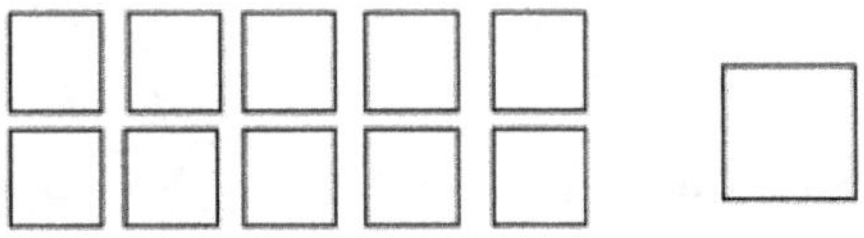

10 decimeters = 1 meter

1000 meters = 1 kilometer

Some of the most commonly used units of measure, centimeters, meters and kilometers are easily interchangeable.

100 centimeters = 1 meter

1 meter = .01 centimeters

1000 meters = 1 kilometer

1 kilometer = .001 meters

Selecting a Unit of Measure

There are different units of measure so that different size objects can be measured appropriately. It would not make sense to measure a paper clip with a kilometer, which is a unit of measure that is most often used to measure long distances. It would also not make sense to measure a long distance with a millimeter or a centimeter, which is a unit of measure that is most often used to measure very small objects.

Millimeter: a very small unit of measure that is used mostly for items such as a the width of a plate or pane of glass

Centimeter: a unit of measure that is very small and is used mostly for item such as a paperclip or how much rain has fallen

Decimeter- a unit of measure that is small and is not commonly used, but can be used for slightly larger objects like a candy bar or a television screen

Meter- a mid-sized unit of measure that is used to measure the size of a room, the height of a building or the length of a truck

Kilometer- a unit of measure that is very large and is used mostly for long distances and heights

Converting Units of Measure

It is sometimes necessary to convert units. If you are working with a very small unit and there are many of them, it may be easier to convert the units to a larger unit.

You may determine that the most appropriate unit of measure is one unit of measure, but when you go to the store to purchase an item, you realize that item is measured using a different unit of measure. You need to be able to easily switch between centimeters, meters and kilometers.

For example, you measure the length of a side to be 1000 centimeters. You get to the store and see that the pieces of wood are being sold by the meter so you convert that to 10 meters.

When converting units of measure, it is important to understand place value. One centimeter is one hundredth (1/100) of a meter and can be represented by 0.01. With an understanding of place value, it is easy to figure out that 10 centimeters are equal to one tenth of a meter and can be represented as 0.1.

For example, 1 kilometer is 1000 meters or 1 kilometer = 0.001. You can then move the decimal point over three places and figure out that 1 meter = 0.001 kilometers.

Another method of converting units of measure is to either multiply or divide. In order to convert a smaller number to a larger number, multiply. In order to convert a larger number to a smaller number, divide.

For example, if 100 centimeters equal 1 meter, in order to figure out how many centimeters are in 2 meters, you would multiply 2 x 100, which equals 200 centimeters.

Length and Area

10 millimeter = 1 centimeter

100 centimeters = 1 meter

1000 meters = 1 kilometer

12 inches = 1 foot

3 feet = 1 yard

1760 yards = 1 mile

Volume

1 milliliter = 1 liter

16 ounces = 1 pint

8 pints = 1 gallon

Length

Length is the distance from one end of an object to the other end of the object. Length is measured using inches, feet, yards, miles, millimeters, centimeters, meters or kilometers.

Perimeter is the distance around the outside of a shape. Perimeter is found by adding together the lengths of all sides of the shape.

Perimeter = side + side (add together as many sides as exist in the shape)

Area

Area is the size of the surface of an object or shape. Area is measured using the same units as length, but in units squared (x^2). Area is found by multiplying the length by width.

Area = length × width

Volume

Volume is the amount that a three-dimensional object can hold or how much space it takes up. Volume is measured with units cubed (x^3). Volume is also measured using ounces, cubic inches or feet, pints, galloons, bushels, cubic centimeters, cubic meters and liters. Volume is found by multiplying length by width by height.

Volume = length × width × height

Time

Time helps us keep track of when to get up, when to go to school, when it's time to eat and many other important things that we do every day. Being able to tell time also allows you to figure out how long you have been doing something. The object that is used to measure time is a clock.

Time is the measurement of the passage of seconds, minutes, hours, days, weeks, months, years and decades. Time is used to keep track of the length of appointments, practices, classes, races, and many other events. Time also helps keep events in chronological order, such as events that happened in the past.

Time can be kept using a 12 hour system or a 24 hour system. In the 12 hour system, midnight is 12:00 and so is noon. In order to tell the difference between 12:00 midnight and 12:00 noon and all of the hours in between, AM (morning) and PM (afternoon) are used.

In the 24 hour system, midnight is 0:00 or 24:00 and noon is 12:00. After noon, the numbers continue to increase: 13:00, 14:00. 15:00, etc. The 24 hour system is most commonly used in the military.

There are two different types of clocks. One is analog and one is digital. The digital clock shows time like this:

An analog clock shows time like this:

The short hand is the hour hand. The longer hand is the minute hand. The long, skinny hand is the second hand.

Most digital clocks only show the hour and the minute. Most analog clocks show the hour, minute and second. Analog clocks have twelve hours represented on them. When telling time with an analog clock, it is important to know whether it is AM or PM. This way, you can tell how long you have been doing something.

For example,

You go to school at 8:30 AM. You leave school at 3:30 PM. You can figure out how long you have been at school by figuring out that you were at school for 3.5 hours in the morning and 3.5 hours in the afternoon. Therefore, you were at school for a total of 7 hours.

Time can be represented on an analog clock, a digital clock or can be written using integers.

For example, eight fifteen and twenty seconds can be represented these two ways:

8:15.20

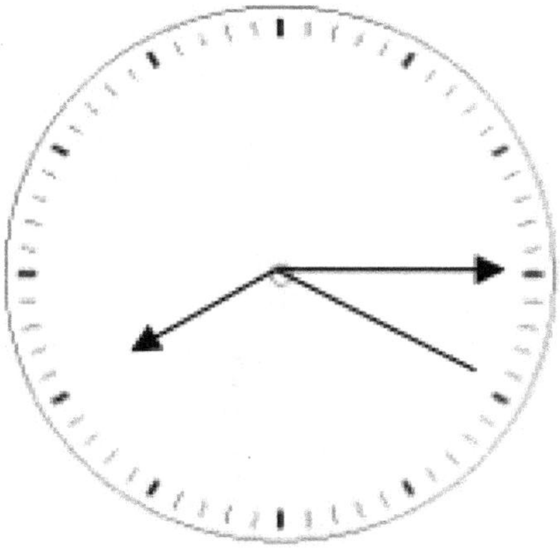

Temperature

Temperature is used to gauge how hot or cold something is. We often talk about temperature when talking about how hot or cold it is outside, in a pool, or in our house. We also talk about temperature changes and how much hotter or colder it has gotten. Temperature affects our daily lives and it is important to be able to accurately measure it.

Temperature can be measured in degrees Celsius, Fahrenheit and Kelvin. Celsius and Fahrenheit are the two most common measurements of temperature.

Both Celsius and Fahrenheit temperature scales have positive and negative numbers. Kelvin temperature scale starts at absolute zero, so it has no negative numbers.

A thermometer is used to measure temperature. Thermometers measure temperature in Kelvin, Celsius or Fahrenheit. The most commonly used measurements of temperature in everyday life are Celsius and Fahrenheit.

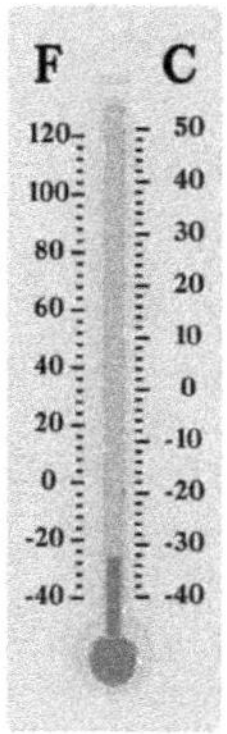

Reading a thermometer is done by looking at the liquid in the thermometer and looking at what number it is next to. The liquid in the thermometer is usually mercury and goes up or down depending on how hot or cold it is. When it is hot, the liquid expands and moves up and when it is cold, the liquid contracts and moves down.

Temperatures are recorded for a variety of reasons. Sometimes it is necessary to figure out a temperature change. For example, when you are sick and you go to the doctor, they take your temperature. If your normal temperature is 98.6 degrees and it is 100.3 degrees when you are sick, the doctor knows that your temperature is about 2 degrees higher than usual. Scientists often measure temperatures when they are doing experiments or to find out the long term effect of something.

Exercises

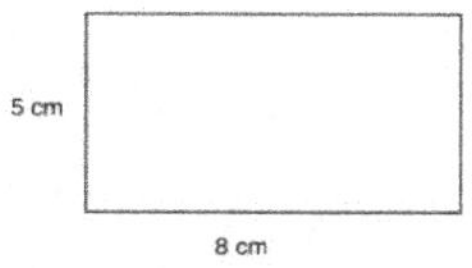

1. Figure out the area of the rectangle. 40 cm²

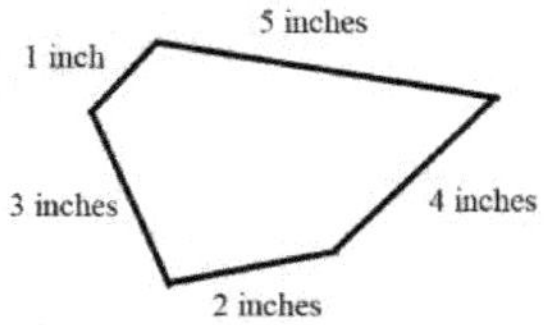

2. What is the perimeter of the pentagon? 15 in

3. Convert 1500 milliliters to liters. 1.5 L

4. How many centimeters are in 1.42 meters? 142

5. What temperature is displayed on the thermometer in Fahrenheit?

100cm = 1 m

1.42 × 100 =

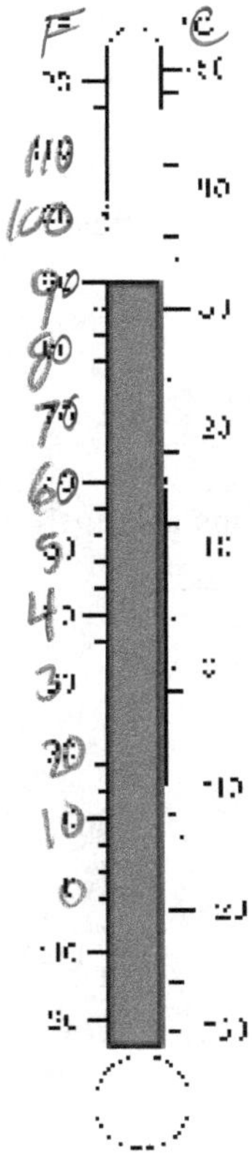

______

6. How many hours pass between 8:45AM and 2:15PM? 5

7. How many kilometers are there in 2000 meters? ______________

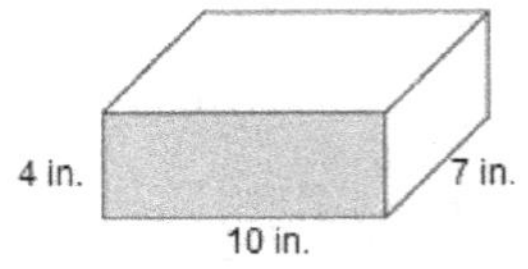

8. Find the volume of the prism. ______________

9. Convert 24 inches to feet. ______________

10. What is the temperature difference between 45 degrees Celsius and 17 degrees Celsius?

____

11. What time is it? ___________

12. What is the perimeter of the octagon that has all equal sides measuring 5 meters?

____

13. How many meters are in 24 kilometers? ______________

14. What is the area of a rectangle that has a length of 8 meters and a width of 12 meters?

____

15. Convert 900 centimeters to meters. ______________

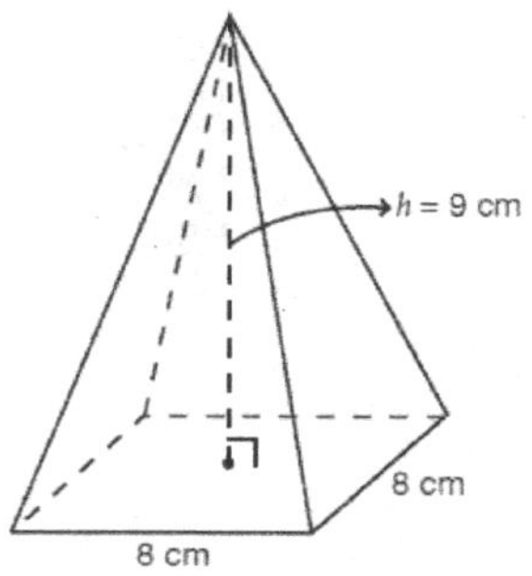

16. Find the volume of the pyramid. ______________

17. How many hours pass between 11PM and 6:45AM? ______________

18. What is the perimeter of the triangle? 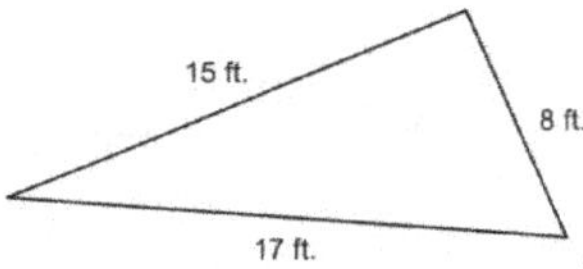

____

19. What is the temperature difference between 13 degrees Celsius and 31 degrees Celsius?

____

20. Convert 8020 centimeters to kilometers. ______________

Quiz

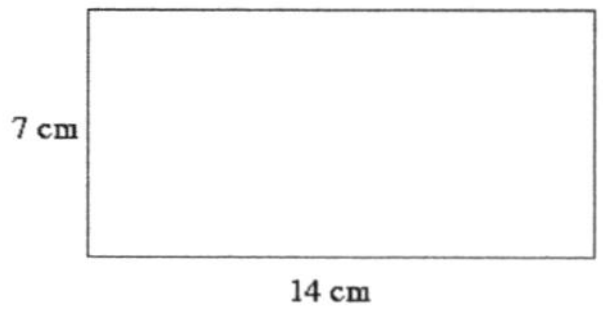

1. Figure out the area of the rectangle. ________________

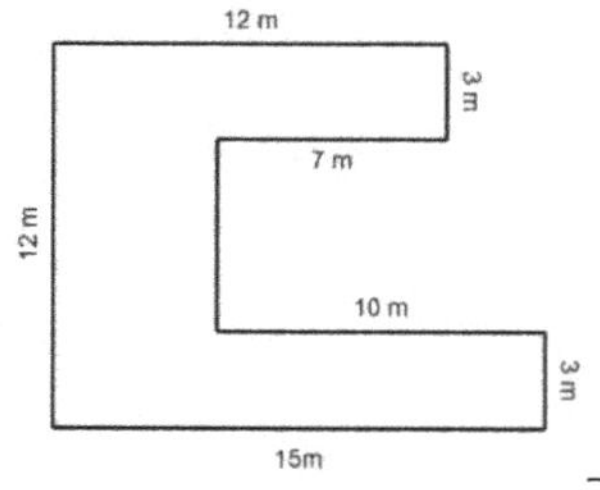

2. What is the perimeter of the polygon? ________________

3. Convert 1.2 liters to milliliters. ________________

4. How many centimeters are in 3.46 meters? ________________

5. What temperature is displayed on the thermometer in Fahrenheit?

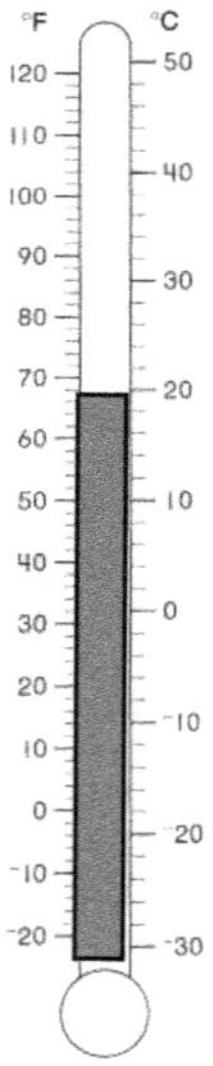

____

6. How many hours pass between 3:15PM and 2:30AM? ________________

7. How many kilometers are there in 5600 meters? ________________

8. Find the volume of the prism. 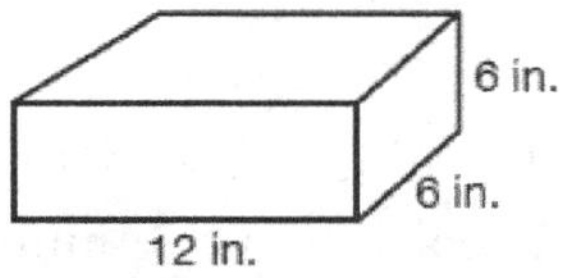

____

9. Convert 21 feet to yards. ____________

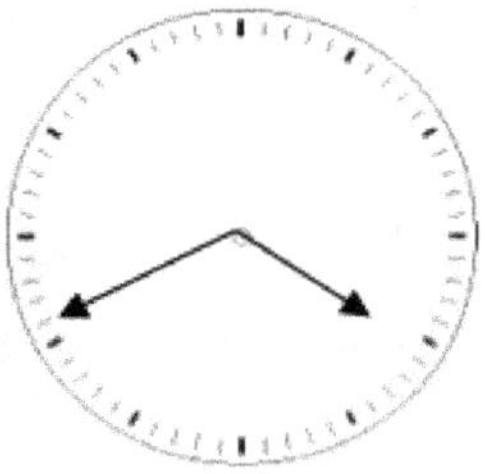

10. What time is it? ____________

Multiplying Large Numbers

Multiplication is an operation that is used for many different reasons. Multiplication is most commonly used when working with larger numbers. Multiplication is used instead of adding the same number multiple times and you find the product. Multiplication can be used with whole numbers, decimals and fractions.

Multiplication

Multiplication is repeated addition. Instead of writing out 5 + 5 + 5 + 5, you would write 5 × 4. The × shows you that you are adding 5 four times. The solution to a multiplication problem is called the product. Using the × symbol is one way to represent a multiplication problem. Another way to represent a multiplication problem is using parentheses. The problem 5 × 4 can also be represented as 5(4). When you see a number in parentheses and a number right next to it, that means to multiply.

There are several different ways that multiplication problems can be represented. One of those ways is with an array model. The array below shows 3 × 6. You can see that there are three rows of six dots each. If you added this up it would be 6 + 6 + 6= 18. You could count all of the dots to find out that there are 18.

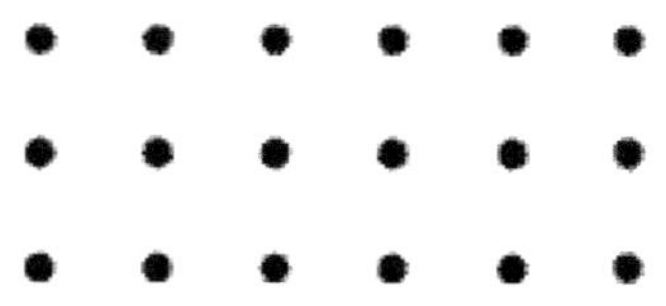

However, using multiplication is much easier because you do not have to add up a lot of numbers or count the dots. Instead, you just multiply 3 × 6.

Another way that multiplication can be represented is with an area model. An area model uses base ten blocks. One cube represents 1 unit. The area model below represents 4 × 3. You can see that there are 4 unit blocks in 3 rows. You can count the blocks and see that there are 12 blocks. It is very easy to see that 4 × 3 = 12.

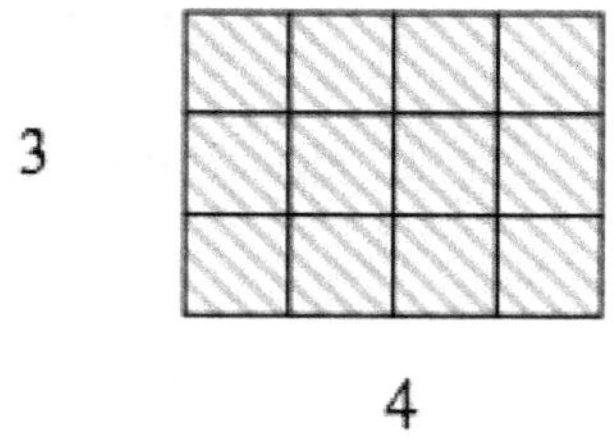

While area and array models are very useful when multiplying small numbers, they are not useful when multiplying large numbers.

Factors

Factors are numbers that can be multiplied together to get another number. For example, $2 \times 3 = 6$. Both 2 and 3 are factors of 6.

Numbers can have many factors, so it is important to think about all of the different numbers that make up the number you are looking at. For example, you know that 2 and 3 are factors of 6, but the numbers 6 and 1 are also factors of 6.

Sometimes you will be asked to find a common factor of two numbers. It is important to figure out all of the factors of each of the numbers. You will then be able to compare the two lists with each other to find the facts that they have in common.

For example,

6: 1, 2, 3, 6

8: 1, 2, 4, 8

The common factors of 6 and 8 are 1 and 2

Fact Families

Fact families have a set of related multiplication and division number sentences.

For example,

$3 \times 5 = 15$

$5 \times 3 = 15$

$15 \div 5 = 3$

$15 \div 3 = 5$

You can see that the number sentences all have the same numbers, but each problem is different. It is very important to learn all of the fact families. Knowing the fact families will make it much easier to do multiplication and division problems!

Factors and fact families are important to understand when working with larger numbers. Both factors and fact families give you a good base for understanding multiplication, which will be incredibly helpful when multiplying larger numbers.

Short Multiplication

Short multiplication can use fact families and factors. Short multiplication is done by lining up the two numbers that you are multiplying vertically.

For example, 2×8 would be written as

$$\begin{array}{r} 2 \\ \times\ 8 \\ \hline \end{array}$$

When multiplying a two or three digit number by a single number, always write the larger number on top.

For example,

$$\begin{array}{r} 654 \\ \times \quad 3 \\ \text{---------} \end{array}$$

To multiply two or three digit numbers that are written vertically, there are several steps.

Step 1: Multiply the single digit number on the bottom by the number directly above it. That number is the number all the way to the right. If the answer to that multiplication problem is more than one digit (for example, 3 × 4), write the number in the ones place.

The digit in the tens place gets carried and written about the tens place.

Step 2: Multiply the single digit number on the bottom by the number in the tens place. If there was a number that was carried, add that to the product of the two numbers. You will again carry the extra digit if there is one and write it above the hundreds place.

Step 3: Continue multiplying the single digit to the numbers above (hundreds place, thousands place, etc.) until all of the numbers have been multiplied.

For example,

$$\begin{array}{r} 654 \\ \times \quad 3 \\ \text{--------} \\ 1962 \end{array}$$

Start by multiplying 3 times 4 to get 12. Write the two below the ones place and carry the extra one to the tens place. Then, multiply 3 by 5 to get 15. You carried a one, so add that to 15. 15 + 1 =16. Write the six below the tens place and carry the one. Last, multiply 3 by 6 to get 18. You carried a one, so add that to 18. 18 + 1 = 19. Write the nine below the hundreds place and the one below the thousands place. That gives you a product of 1962.

Long Multiplication

Long multiplication is used when multiplying two numbers that have more than one digit each. An example of the type of problem for which long multiplication would be used is 54 × 385.

Long multiplication involves the same steps as short multiplication. However, there are many additional steps for long multiplication. Just like with short multiplication, when writing the multiplication problem down vertically, the larger number goes above the smaller number. It is very important that the smallest digits in both numbers are lined up.

For example,

```
  385
 × 54
------------
```

The first steps in long multiplication are the same as short multiplication. Multiply the digit in the ones place with the numbers above it. Remember to carry any digits to the next place. After multiplying the first digit in the bottom number, use the following steps.

Step 1: Under the answer from the digit from the first digits answer, write a zero under the ones place.

Step 2: Multiply the digit in the tens place on the bottom just like you did the digit in the ones place. If the answer to that multiplication problem is more than one digit (for example, 3 ×

4), write the number in the ones place. The digit in the tens place gets carried and written about the tens place.

Step 3: Multiply the digit in the tens place on the bottom by the number in the tens place. If there was a number that was carried, add that to the product of the two numbers. You will again carry the extra digit if there is one and write it above the hundreds place.

Step 4: Continue multiplying the single digit to the numbers above (hundreds place, thousands place, etc.) until all of the numbers have been multiplied.

Step 5: Once all of the numbers have been multiplied, add together the products. The sum of the products is your answer.

For example,

```
   385
 × 54
------------
  1540
+ 19250
------------
 20790
```

Start by multiplying 4 times 5 to get 20. Write the zero below the ones place and carry the extra two to the tens place. Then, multiply 4 by 8 to get 32. You carried a two, so add that to 32. 32 + 2 =34. Write the four below the tens place and carry the three. Last, multiply 4 by 3 to get 12. You carried a three, so add that to 12. 12 + 3 = 15. Write the five below the hundreds place and the one below the thousands place. That gives you a product of 1540.

Next, write a zero below the ones place. Then, multiply 5 by 5 to get 25. Write the 5 below the tens place and carry the two. Then, multiply 5 by 8 to get 40. You carried a two, so add that to 40. 40 + 2 = 42. Write the two in the hundreds place and carry the four. Last, multiply 5 by 3 to get 15. You carried a four so add that to 15. 15 + 4 = 19. Write the nine in the thousands place and the one in the ten thousands place.

Then, add the products together. 1540 + 19250= 20790. That is the answer to your multiplication problem.

Remember, the same steps apply no matter how many digits are used. However, EVERY TIME you multiply another digit, you will add that many zeros before you begin multiplying.

For example, when you multiply a number in the ones place by the number above, you add no zeros. When you multiply a number in the tens place by the number above, you add one zero. When you multiply a number in the hundreds place by the number above, you add two zeros.

Decimals

Decimals can easily be multiplied. The same steps are used when multiplying decimals as when multiplying whole numbers. Always line the numbers u so that the smallest places are in line. Multiply the numbers without worrying about the decimal point. At the end, after you have added the sums to get the answer, then the decimal point comes back into play. Count the number of decimals places that there are.

For example, in the number 8.15 there are two decimal places (the numbers to the right of the decimal point.)

You will then look at the answer and count from the right over that number of places. The decimal point will then be put there.

For example, if the answer is 579234 and there are two decimal places, count over from the right two places and put the decimal point. The answer would then be 5792.34

Exercises

1. 452 × 3	2. 843 × 7	3. 1294 × 5
4. 789 × 6	5. 1370 × 8	6. 6208 × 6
7. 1275 × 12	8. 5714 × 31	9. 1982 × 18
10. 567 × 23	11. 871 × 24	12. 8113 × 44
13. 3012 × 11	14. 3124 × 121	15. 1286 × 307
16. 7823 × 202	17. 4506 × 247	18. 6062 × 314
19. 2879 × 403	20. 9126 × 321	

Quiz

1. 583×7
2. 719×4
3. 2013×3
4. 827×15
5. 4099×18
6. 1753×24
7. 2591×347
8. 1277×233
9. 874×503
10. 6183×782

Probability

Probability is the chance that something will happen or the likelihood that some event will happen. Probability is used in many different circumstances such as meteorology, dice games, and sporting events. Probability is not definite, so probability cannot be used to conclusively predict the outcome of an event. Instead, probability gives us an idea about what could happen.

Probability is often measured with a number and is most often represented by a percent or a fraction. Sometimes only words are used when talking about probability are impossible, unlikely, possible, even change, likely and certain. For example, a meteorologist may predict that there is a 30% chance that it will rain or it is unlikely that it will rain.

In situations such as tossing a coin or rolling dice, probability is the best way to figure out what might happen. When you toss a coin, there is a 50% chance that it will land on heads. Another way to state that is there is a 1 out of 2 or ½ chance that it will land on heads.

When rolling a dice, there are six possible numbers that could come up. That means that there is a 1 out of 6 chance that you will get any of those numbers or a 17% chance.

Representing Probability

Probability can be represented using words or it can be represented as a percent or a fraction. To represent the probability of an outcome as a percent, the fraction needs to be figured out first. Representing probability as a fraction can be explained in general terms. Probability equals the number of ways that something can happen divided by the total number of outcomes that are possible.

$$\text{Probability} = \frac{\text{Number of ways something can happen}}{\text{Total number of outcomes}}$$

Once you have a fraction, you can easily figure out the likelihood of an event in a percent. To do that, use the following steps.

Step 1: Divide the denominator (the bottom number or total number of outcomes) into the numerator (the top number or number of ways that something can happen.

Step 2: Take the decimal that you came up with and move the decimal point to the right two places.

Step 3: Put a percent sign next to the whole number on the right side.

For example, you have a bag of 9 marbles. 5 of them are red and 4 of them are blue. You want to figure out the probability of you choosing a red marble. The probability of you choosing a red marble is 5/9. There are 5 red marbles, so that is the number of ways something could happen. There are 9 total marbles so that is the total number of outcomes. If you wanted to turn the fraction into a percent, you would divide 5 by 9 to get .55. To make the decimal into a percent, move the decimal point over to the right two places. The probability in a percent would be 55%.

Another example is you have a bag of 15 discs. The discs are red, yellow and blue and there are five of each color. You want to figure out the probability of you choosing a red or a yellow disc. There are 5 red and 5 yellow discs. You add those together to get 10. So you know the probability of choosing a red or a yellow disc is 10/15. There are ten red and yellow discs which is the number of ways that something could happen. There are a total of 15 discs so that is the total number of outcomes. If you wanted to turn the fraction into a percent, you would divide 10 by 15 to get .66. To make the decimal into a percent, move the decimal point over to the right two places. The probability in a percent would be 66%.

Probability Line

A probability line is another way that probability can be represented. Once the probability of something is known, it can be placed on a line.

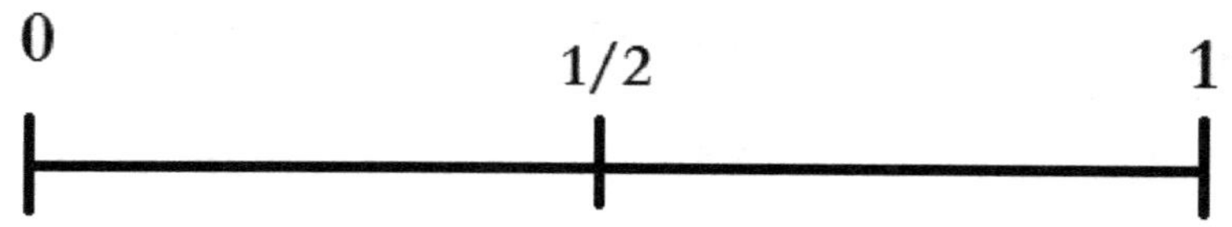

On the probability line, something that is placed at zero is an impossible event. For something that is placed at ½, there is an even chance. Something that is placed at one is a certain event.

For example, a meteorologist may look at the radar and see that there is a big storm coming. He would then report that there will definitely be rain. He would put the chance of rain at the 1 on the probability line because he is certain it will rain.

The probability line is really helpful when you are trying to figure out the probability of many different events. After you figure out the probability, you can place each event on the probability line. You can then go back and reference the probability line to compare the events or answer any questions that may need answers.

Results of Experiments

A probability experiment is simply when an event is measured for the possible outcomes. Once you have figured out what the probability of an event is, you can use the results of the probability experiment to help make predictions.

Remember, the results of a probability experiment are just a guideline. There is no completely accurate way to predict results. However, you can use the results of a probability experiment to help you indicate what may or what could happen. After you have determined the probability, you can then make an educated guess about the outcome of something.

For example, if your probability experiment indicates that there is a 5/7 chance that you will get a puppy, you can predict that you will be getting a puppy. You could make that educated guess based on the fact that 5/7 is more than half. If you were to change 5/7 to a percentage, it would 71%. When something has more than an even chance or a 50/50 chance, you can predict that the event is more likely to happen.

Another example is that your probability experiment indicates that there is 42% chance that you will get to go on vacation with your best friend. With those results, you can make an educated guess that it is unlikely you will be able to go. You can make that prediction because 42% is less than 50%. When something is less than 50%, you can predict that the event is unlikely to happen.

Possible Outcomes

In addition to figuring out the likelihood of an event happening, probability is also used to figure out all of the possible outcomes of an event. While understanding the chance that something will happen is helpful, it can be even more helpful to be able to see all of the possible outcomes of an event.

For example, you are spinning a spinner one time that has four colors, red, yellow, blue and green. You know that the possibility of spinning the spinner one time and landing on green is ¼ or 25%. So, all of the possible outcomes are red, yellow, blue and green.

The possible outcomes in a situation like that are very basic and really do not need to be listed. However, in a more complicated situation, it would be helpful to list all of the possible outcomes.

For example, there is a jar that has 23 marbles. There are 6 yellow marbles, 8 red marbles, 4 white marbles, 3 purple marbles and 1 blue marbles. You want to know what the probability of choosing each different color marble is if you choose one marble at a time and replace the marbles when you are done. To figure that out, you need to list all of the possible outcomes.

Yellow marble= 6/23

Red marble= 8/23

White marble= 4/23

Purple marble= 3/23

Blue marble= 1/23

Listing all of these possible outcomes is useful so that you can figure out the likelihood of choosing each color. You could even plot each of these possibilities on a probability line. You would then be able to compare the likelihood of each event.

When listing all of the possible outcomes, you still need to figure out the probability of each event. You will then look at all of the possible outcomes to see the full picture of what could possibly happen. You can look at each possibility individually or you can compare them. You will also be able to easily work with each possibility.

For example, using the marbles in a jar example, you wanted to figure out the probability that you would choose a primary color. You already have all of the possible outcomes listed. You know the probability of choosing a yellow marble is 6/23, the probability of choosing a red marble is 8/23 and the probability of choosing a blue marble is 1/23. You can add each of those together and easily figure out the probability of choosing a primary color. $6 + 8 + 1 = 15$. The probability of choosing a primary color is 15/23.

While listing each possible outcome is more time consuming to do, having all of the possible outcomes makes is much easier to answer questions and work with the probability event.

Exercises

1. If there are 8 colors on a color wheel, what is the probability of landing on each individual color?

   ____

2. What is the probability, in a percentage, of 3/8? __________

3. If there is a 2/5 chance of something happening, what is the likelihood that it will happen?

   ____

4. There is a 1/6 chance that you will roll a 1, 2, 3, 4, 5, or 6 when rolling a dice. What is the probability that you will roll an odd number? __________

5. Place the following probability outcomes on the probability line: 1/9, 5/9, 9/9

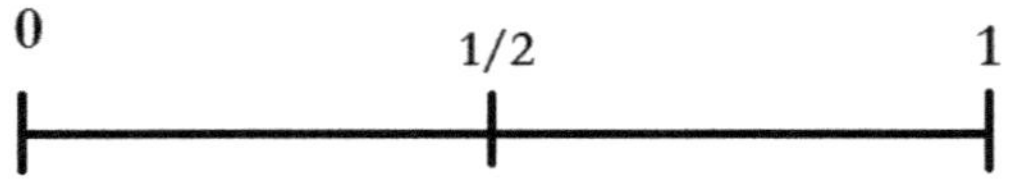

6. There are 14 baseballs in the bag, 9 footballs, 5 soccer balls and 18 tennis balls. List all of the possible outcomes for the type of ball that one could get when reaching into the bag.

   ____

   ____

   ____

7. If there is a 25% chance of rain, what is the likelihood that it will rain? __________

8. There are 15 marbles in a jar with an equal number of pink, teal and purple marbles. What is the probability of getting a pink marble? __________

9. What is the probability, in a percentage, of 7/11? __________

10. There is a 1/5 chance of choosing a brownie, cookie, slice of pie, slice of cake or pudding. What is the probability that you will choose a slice of something?

    ____

11. There are 6 compliments are written on pink pieces of paper, 11 compliments are written on blue pieces of paper and 8 compliments are written white pieces of paper in a compliment jar. List all of the possible outcomes for the color paper that one will get when reaching into the jar to pull out a compliment.

    ____

    ____

____

12. There are 16 clownfish, 23 angelfish, 11 anemone and 19 seahorses in an aquarium. Which fish are you most likely to get if you reach in? __________

13. If there is a 80% chance that you will pass a test, what is the likelihood of passing? __________

14. Place the following probability outcomes on the probability line: 3/15, 7/15, 14/15

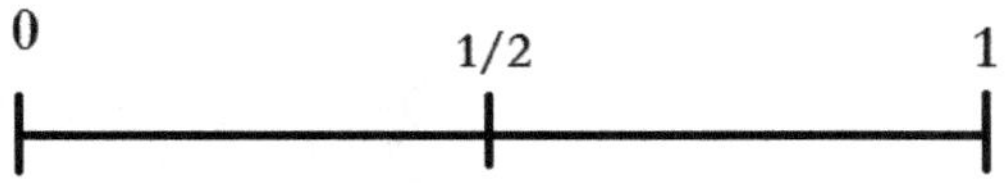

15. There are 36 pets in the shelter. Half are dogs and 1/3 are cats. What is the probability you will choose a cat? __________

16. What is the probability, in a percentage, of 9/27 __________

17. There are 26 daisies, 13 roses, 17 irises, and 23 carnations in one container. What is the probability that you will pull out a rose when you reach in the container? __________

18. If there is a 48% chance of winning the game, what is the likelihood that you will win the game?

____

19. There are 11 chocolate donuts, 17 plain donuts and 22 glazed donuts in a box. List all of the possible outcomes for the type of donut that one will get when taking one out of the box.

____

____

____

20. There are 62 cans of paint. 24 are white, 17 are pink and the rest are purple. What is the probability you will choose a purple can? __________

Quiz

1. If there are 12 colors on a color wheel, what is the probability of landing on each individual color?
   ____

2. What is the probability, in a percentage, of 6/14? __________

3. If there is a 4/8 chance of something happening, what is the likelihood that it will happen?
   ____

4. There is a 1/6 chance that you will roll a 1, 2, 3, 4, 5, or 6 when rolling a dice. What is the probability that you will roll a number less than 4? __________

5. Place the following probability outcomes on the probability line: 0/7, 4/7, 6/7

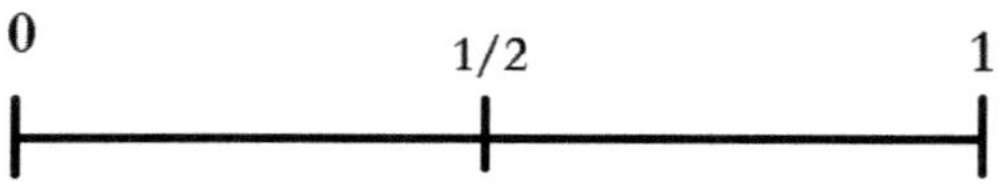

6. Mark has different uniforms for his job. He has 7 white shirts, 9 blue shirts and 12 striped shirts. List all of the possible outcomes for the type of shirt that Mark could get when he reaches in his uniform drawer.

   ____

   ____

   ____

7. If there is a 85% chance of rain, what is the likelihood that it will rain? __________

8. There are 25 marbles in a jar with an equal number of orange, blue, white, green and yellow marbles. What is the probability of getting an orange marble? __________

9. What is the probability, in a percentage, of 6/18? __________

10. There is a 1/6 chance of getting a vanilla, chocolate, twist, raspberry, peanut butter or blackberry ice cream cone. What is the probability that you will choose a berry flavored ice cream cone?
    ____

Whole Numbers

Whole numbers are digits that have no decimals or fractional parts. Whole numbers are numbers 0, 1, 2, 3... Whole numbers are always positive numbers. Whole numbers can also be called counting numbers because they are the numbers that you use when counting objects. It is easy to remember that whole numbers are always positive when you think about counting. You ever count using negative numbers, only positive numbers.

Integers are very similar to whole numbers, but they also include negative numbers, such as -4, -3, -2, -1, 0, 1, 2, 3.... Like whole numbers, integers do not have decimal or fractional parts. Sometimes the words integer and whole numbers are used interchangeably. However, there is a difference between whole numbers and integers!

Whole numbers are used in addition, subtraction, multiplication and division. They are also able to be estimated and rounded. There is not a lot that cannot be done with whole numbers. Whole numbers are the most commonly used numbers in math and are the easiest numbers to work with.

Standard, Expanded and Written Form

A number that is written in standard form is written with digits. Standard form can also be called numeral form since you are simply writing the numerals. For example, the number 561 written in standard form is 561.

A number that is written in expanded form is written in a way that shows the value of each digit in the number. For example, the number 561 would be written as 500 + 60 + 1. In order to write a number in expanded form, you must have an understanding of place value. You must understand that the 5 in the number 561 is in the hundreds place and can be represented as 500. You must understand that the 6 in the number 561 is in the tens place and can be represented as 60. The number in the ones place is written just the way it is. All of those numbers are then written as an addition statement.

Written form is when a number is written out with words. Written form is primarily used when writing out checks. For example, 561 would be written as five hundred sixty one.

Standard, expanded and written form can all be used to represent whole numbers.

Place Value

Place value is what allows us to look at a number and figure out if it is big or small. Place value is the position of a digit in a number and its value. Place value helps us to understand a numbers relationship to the other numbers as well as to be able to identify very large or very small numbers.

Place value is a system of representation in which the position of a number with respect to a point, or decimal point, determines its value. In whole numbers, the decimal point is often not shown. Rather, the decimal point is assumed because it is not necessary to the value of the number. In whole numbers, it can be assumed that the decimal point is after or to the right of the ones place.

The example below shows a very large number. Knowing place value will help you to identify the value of each digit. Place value will also be incredibly helpful when comparing or ordering numbers as you will need to identify the smallest number and the largest number. Without place value, that would not be possible.

4	8	2	3	8	1	8	2	0	2	4	7
Hundred Billions	Ten Billions	Billions	Hundred Millions	Ten Millions	Millions	Hundred thousands	Ten thousands	Thousands	Hundreds	Tens	Ones

Operations

Addition, subtraction, multiplication and division are all used for a variety of different reasons. Addition is used when combining several numbers together to find a sum. Subtraction is used when taking numbers away from each other to find the difference. Multiplication is used instead of adding the same number multiple times and you find the product. Division is used when dividing one number multiple times and you find the quotient.

When solving problems involving whole numbers, it is important to be able to identify what operation is most useful. In order to successfully do that, you need to have a good understanding of what each of the operations does. All of the operations, addition, subtraction, multiplication and division, can be used with whole numbers, decimals and fractions.

When adding and subtracting, it is very important to remember to line up the places for numbers that have multiple digits in them. For example, the ones place must be lined up with the ones place and the tens place must be lined up with the tens place if adding 14 to 19.

Factor Pairs

A factor pair is a set of two numbers that when multiplied together make the number that is being factored. For example, the factors of 18 are: 1, 2, 3, 6, 9, 18. The factor pairs are 1 and 18, 2 and 9 and 3 and 6.

Another example is the factors of 21 are 1, 3, 7, 21. The factor pairs are 1 and 21 and 3 and 7.

Factor pairs are always made up of whole numbers and can be used when solving problems involving whole numbers. Factor pairs are most useful when solving multiplication or division problems.

Rounding

Rounding is when a number is made into a number that is easier to work with. This is done by keeping the value of the number the same, but decreasing the number of digits. The number of digits that you work with when rounding is decreased by making some of the digits in the number into zeros. When rounding, you will either increase or decrease a number based on place value. Using numbers that have been rounded results in an answer that is not as accurate as if you were using the actual numbers, which must be kept in mind!

To round a number, you first need to know what place you are rounding to. You then need to look at the place to the right of the place you are rounding to.

For example, if you are told to round to the nearest ten, you will look at the ones place. If the number is smaller than 5, you will round the number down. If the number is 5 or larger, you will round the number up.

When rounding to the nearest hundred, look at the tens place. When rounding to the nearest thousand, look at the hundreds place.

Rounding is useful when you are trying to estimate numbers that are very large. Rounding in an easy way to shorten the number and make it easier to work with.

Estimation

Estimation is making an educated guess based on your knowledge of the operation you are using. Estimation is used with addition, subtraction, multiplication and division. For example, when using addition, you know that you are trying to find out to total when the numbers are put together. When using subtraction, you know that you are trying to find out the total when one number is taken away from another number.

When estimating, you are not trying to get an exact answer; you are just trying to find an approximate answer.

For example, 78 + 62 = approximately 140. The answer is found by rounding the two numbers that are being added together. 78 rounds to 80 and 62 rounds to 60. So, you would add 80 + 60 =140.

Estimation is most often used when shopping, but can be used in many different situations. Estimation is really useful because it can be done in your head.

For example, when you are shopping, you can estimate the total your purchase will be. This is incredibly helpful because you may not have paper and a pencil with you or even want to take the time to add up all of your purchases to find the exact total. Estimating the total can help you be prepared when you purchase your items.

Prime and Composite Numbers

Whole numbers can be described as either prime or composite. A prime number is a number that can only be divided evenly by itself or 1. That means that prime numbers only have two factors. Prime numbers are always whole numbers that are greater than 1. Some examples of prime numbers are 11, 17, and 19.

A composite number is a number that have many factors. It can be divided evenly by more than just itself and 1. Composite numbers are always whole numbers that are greater than 1. Some examples of composite numbers are 12, 25 and 36.

It is important to know or be able to identify which whole numbers are prime and while are composite. When multiplying or dividing, it is often necessary to know of a number is prime or composite. If a number is prime, it will not be able to be divided by any numbers other than 1 and itself. It is also helpful to identify a number as prime or composite when listing the factors of a number.

Exercises

1. Is 9 a prime or composite number? __________
2. Round the answer to 92 + 16 __________
3. What are the factors pairs for 24? _________________________
4. What is the value of 7 in the number 821,734? __________
5. Estimate the answer to 88 ÷ 9 __________
6. Write the number 682 in expanded form _______________
7. Round the answer to 116 – 43 __________
8. Is 23 a prime or composite number? __________
9. What are the factor pairs for 30? ___________
10. Write the number 430 in written form ______________
11. Estimate the answer to 103 × 5 __________
12. Round the answer to 73 + 29 __________
13. What are the factors of 66? __________
14. What is the value of 3 in the number 9,302,145? __________
15. Write the number 7832 in expanded form _______________
16. Round the answer to 93 – 12 __________
17. Is 86 prime or composite? __________
18. Estimate the answer to 67 + 43 + 19 __________
19. What are the factor pairs for 40? ___________
20. What is the value of 5 in the number 8,645,023? __________

Quiz

1. Is 15 a prime or composite number? __________
2. Round the answer to $97 \div 5$ __________
3. What are the factors pairs for 32? __________
4. What is the value of 2 in the number 298,539? __________
5. Estimate the answer to $34 + 15 + 89$ __________
6. Write the number 989 in expanded form __________
7. Round the answer to $832 - 513$ __________
8. Is 31 a prime or composite number? __________
9. What are the factor pairs for 42? __________
10. Write the number 781 in written form __________

Word Problems

Word problems are math problems that are presented in sentence form. It is often necessary to create an equation to figure out the problem. Word problems can involve any type of mathematical operation and any type of number.

When solving word problems, it is very important to read all of the words carefully and then figure out which information is important. There are many steps to follow when solving word problems.

Step 1: Read the word problem very carefully

Step 2: Figure out what information the word problem is asking you to figure out

Step 3: Figure out what information in the word problem is not necessary to solving the problem

Step 4: Draw a diagram to help you picture the problem. This step is not always necessary, but if it will help, do it!

Step 5: Write out the math problem that is described in the word Problem

Step 6: Solve the problem and write down the answer. If the answer includes any specific units such as feet or centimeters, be sure to include those units with your answer.

Solving word problems can be more complicated than solving traditional math problems that are written in numeral form. However, if all of the steps are followed, solving word problems can be a lot of fun!

Addition, Subtraction, Multiplication and Division Word Problems

Many word problems will require you to use the standard math operations, addition, subtraction, multiplication and division. There are some key words that are used in word problems to help you identify which operation should be used.

Key words that are used in addition problems are add, altogether, both, in all, sum, and, more, extra, combined and total. All of those words are about bringing two objects or numbers together. When you see these key words or other similar words, remember to add.

Key words that are used in subtraction problems are difference, fewer, left, less, minus, decrease, reduce and remains. All of these words are about taking objects or numbers away from each other. When you see these key words or other similar words, remember to subtract.

Key words that are used in multiplication problems are times, every, product, of, as much, twice, by and at this rate. All of these words are about increasing objects or a number many times. When you see these key words or other similar words, remember to multiply.

Key words that are used in division problems are each, divide evenly, split, every, average, out of and shared. All of these words are about dividing or splitting up objects or numbers. When you see these key words or other similar words, remember to divide.

For example, Thomas works at a clothing store. He has to put out 114 shirts on 6 different tables. How many shirts will he put on each table? This example has the word each in it, which is a key word for division. You will then write the problem out. $114 \div 6 =$ Solve the problem. $114 \div 6 = 19$. Then, rewrite the answer so that it has the units next to it. Thomas will put 19 shirts on each table.

Some word problems may involve estimation and rounding. Those word problems will tell you to estimate or round the answer. Look for the same key words that you look for in addition, subtraction, multiplication and division problems, but remember to either estimate or round the answer.

Decimal and Fraction Word Problems

Word problems involving decimals and fractions will be written much like addition, subtraction, multiplication and division problems. All of the same operations will be used with decimals and fractions that are used with whole numbers.

Look for the same key words that you would look for in word problems involving each of the operations. The most important thing to remember when solving word problems involving decimals and fractions is to treat the decimals and fractions just like you would if you were solving a word problem involving only numerals. When adding and subtracting decimals, remember to keep the places lined up. When multiplying and dividing decimals, remember to count the number of decimal places and include those in your answer. When working with fractions, remember that when adding and subtracting, the denominators must be the same. Remember to reduce your answer where possible when multiplying and dividing fractions.

For example, Kristie is making cookies for a surprise party. There will be a lot of people there so Kristie needs to triple the recipe. The original recipe calls for ¼ cup of sugar. How much sugar does Kristie need now? To solve this problem, you need to multiply ¼ by 3, which can also be represented as 3/1. Multiply the numerators 1 × 3 to get 3 and multiply the denominators 4 × 1 to get 4. Write the numerator over the denominator to get ¾ cup of sugar.

Geometry Word Problems

When solving word problems involving geometry, drawing a diagram can be incredibly helpful. Drawing a diagram can help you to visualize the shape that is being described. Shapes and angles that are described in word problems may not be easy to visualize. That is why it is important to read the problems very carefully to ensure that you completely understand the shape or angle that is being described.

For example, which shape has 6 sides, 6 acute angles and is two dimensional? This word problem is easier to solve if a diagram is drawn. If you draw a two dimensional shape with 6 sides, you will have a hexagon. After you draw that shape, check to make sure that all of the angles are acute. If they are, you know the answer is hexagon.

Probability Word Problems

Word problems involving probability will have a scenario explained. It is then very important to figure out what answer the word problem is looking for. Sometimes you may need to find the probability of the scenario in a fraction and sometimes you may need to find the probability of the scenario in a percentage. It is also possible that you may need to list all of the possible outcomes of the scenario that is described.

For example, Caroline is baking cookies. She bakes 32 chocolate chip cookies, 28 peanut butter cookies and 36 oatmeal raisin cookies. What is the probability that you will get a peanut butter cookie from the tray where she has all of the cookies? In order to find the probability, you need to first figure out the total number of cookies. 32 + 28 + 36 = 96 cookies. Then, you can write the probability as a fraction 28/96 or as a percentage 29%.

Measurement Word Problems

Word problems involving measurements such as volume, area and perimeter will have a lot of information in them. To keep track of the information, it is sometimes helpful to draw a diagram. Often times in word problems involving measurements, the measurements of sides or angles are provided. Drawing a diagram will allow you to write in all of the measurements provided so that you will better be able to see what information is missing.

When solving measurement word problems, it is also very important to remember all of the different formulas. Perimeter is found by adding all of the sides together. Area of a square or rectangle is length × width. Area of a triangle is 1/2base × height. Volume is length × width × height. Based on the information provided, it may be necessary for you to figure out what formula to use. That is why it is so important to read all of the information in the word problems.

For example, you are building a fence around your yard. The lengths are 8 feet, 12 feet, 6 feet and 9 feet. What is the perimeter? You could draw a picture of a polygon with four sides and label each side if that will help you. To find the perimeter, you must add all of the sides together. 8 + 12 + 6 + 9 = 35 feet.

Word problems involving temperature and time will require you to read the problem carefully and eliminate any information that is not needed. You will then be able to solve the problem.

For example, you place an online order for 3 new games. You place the order on Tuesday at 3:15 PM. You get the games delivered to you on Friday at 4:55 PM. How much time went by between when you placed the order and got your games? You know that you can eliminate the information about the online order for 3 new games because it does not matter to the problem. You also know that you have to find a time difference, which means you will subtract. 4:55 – 3:15 is what you need to figure out. 3:15 to 4:15 is one hour. 4:15 to 4:55 can be found by subtracting 55 – 15 = 40. You know the answer is 1 hour and 40 minutes.

Algebra Word Problems

Word problems that involve algebra can some of the most difficult word problems to solve. In addition to reading and understanding the word problem, you also need to identify the unknown. Once you have identified what unknown you will be finding, you will need to identify the operation that is being used.

Writing out the equation as you are reading the word problem can be very helpful. Before solving the equation, it is important to go back and reread the word problem to check and make sure that you understood what was being asked. You can then solve the problem for the unknown. Remember to include any units of measure after you answer if needed.

For example, Nathan has 7 bundles of sticks. Each bundle has 14 sticks in it. He wants to the total number of sticks he has. First start by figuring out the unknown. You do not know the total number of sticks. Write the equation $7 \times 14 = x$. Then, solve for x by multiplying 7 and 14. $x = 98$. Then, write the answer using the units. 98 sticks

Exercises

1. Jeremy is spending his summer mowing lawns. He has 13 different lawns that he is responsible for mowing. He gets paid $12 for each lawn that he mows. Week 1, Jeremy mows 6 lawns. How much does he make? __________

2. Carrie loves to scrapbook. She uses stickers to help make her scrapbook pages more colorful. Carrie uses about 4 stickers per page. There are 18 pages in Carrie's scrapbook. Estimate how many stickers she used in her scrapbook? __________

3. Roger goes fishing. He catches 15 bass. He likes to share his fish with his friends. He divides his fish between 5 people. Write an equation and then solve to figure out how many fish each person will get. __________

4. I am three-dimensional. I have no right angles, no parallel lines and no perpendicular lines. I could roll. Who am I? __________

5. Justin fixes heaters. When he gets to a house with no heat he takes the temperature. He measured the temperature as 63.8°. After he fixed the heater and the heat went on, he measured the temperature as 72.9°. How much did the temperature rise? __________

6. You have a friend who moves to Hawaii. It is 7:13 at night and you really want to call your friend to talk to him. His time zone is 3 hours behind yours. What time is it where your friend is? __________

7. There are three color plates that are used in the cafeteria. There are 100 yellow plates, 50 green plates and 50 blue plates. What is the probability that you will get a green plate? __________

8. There are 90 dresses. You have tried on $^1/_4$ of them. Write an equation and then solve to figure out how many dresses you have tried on. __________

9. Ralph has a toy that is a regular hexagon. The sides are an even number. He figures out that the perimeter of the hexagon is 24 inches, but he wants to know how long each of the sides are. __________

10. I am three-dimensional. I have 2 pairs of parallel lines and 4 right angles. My faces meet at one point on top. Who am I? __________

11. Pat loves to play sports. He has a bag of balls in his garage. There are 14 baseballs in the bag, 9 footballs, 5 soccer balls and 18 tennis balls. List all of the possible outcomes for the type of ball that Pat could get when he reaches in his bag. ____________________

12. There are 38 spoons to be washed. You have done half. Write an equation and then solve to figure out the total number of spoons you washed. __________

13. Sally needs to know the volume of a container that is 14 centimeters tall. The length and width are half of the height. What is the volume? __________

14. Mr. Smith is making brownies for his class. He is making two batches. The original recipe calls for 1/3 cup of oil. How much oil does he need now? __________

15. Sebastian, Hank, Theresa and Josie all kept track of the snowfall in their city for the month of January. Sebastian's city got 35.269 inches of snow in January. Hank's city got 5 thousandths more than Sebastian's city. How much snow did his city get? __________

16. Which shape has 4 sides of different lengths, 4 right angles and is two dimensional? __________

17. Joe is playing a ball pit. There are 78 yellow balls, 93 red balls and 84 blue balls. What is the probability that he will pick up a yellow ball when he reaches all the way down to the bottom of the ball pit? __________

18. Sebastian, Hank, Theresa and Josie all kept track of the snowfall in their city for the month of January. Sebastian's city got 35.269 inches of snow in January. Theresa's city got 4.02 more inches of snow than Hank's city. How much snow did her city get? __________

19. Jaclyn babysits 3 days a week. She makes $11 an hour. If she babysat for 9 hours one week, how much money did she make? __________

20. Tim shops and buys items that cost $6.78, $11.32 and $23.45. Round the cost of the items to figure how about how much he will spend. __________

Quiz

1. Ilene is an artist. She makes ceramic bowls and sells them at craft fairs. Ilene has 27 bowls to bring with her to the craft fair on Saturday. At the craft fair, Ilene sells all of her bowls. Ilene also gets orders for 19 bowls. It takes Ilene 3 hours to make each bowl. How long will it take her to make the bowls that were ordered? __________

2. Henry is helping at a spaghetti dinner. He is in charge of making the juice. Henry has to use 13 gallons of water to make the juice every half an hour. After 3 hours, estimate how many gallons of water will Henry have used? __________

3. Pam loves to paint. She has 56 different color paints. Pam wants to put her paints in containers. The containers only hold 8 colors each. Write an equation and then solve to figure out how many containers will Pam need? __________

4. You are learning to scuba dive. You start in waters that are 62.6° As you start to dive down the water gets colder. It is 11.7° colder where you dive than it is at the surface. What is the temperature of the water you are diving in? __________

5. You are timing a race. The first person passes the finish line in 23 minutes and 16 seconds. The last person passes the finish line in 37 minutes and 29 seconds. How much faster was the first person than the last person? __________

6. Your teacher has 5 different types of stickers that she puts on completed homework. She has 15 smiley faces, 20 flowers, 20 hearts, 15 stars and 25 animals. What is the probability that you will get a heart sticker on your paper? __________

7. There are 58 photos printed. You have to print 3 times more. Write an equation and then solve to figure out how many photos total you have to print. __________

8. Kyle is planning a senior prank. He is going to cover the football field with spray paint. He knows the area of a field is 121 meters^2. The sides of the field are the same. Kyle needs to know what the lengths of the sides of the field are so that he can make sure he has enough people on each side to get the field completely covered. __________

9. Kristie is making cookies for a surprise party. There will be a lot of people there so Kristie needs to triple the recipe. The original recipe calls for ½ tsp. baking soda. How much baking soda does Kristie need now? __________

10. I am three-dimensional. I have 6 faces and 6 pairs of parallel lines. Each face has right angles. All of my faces are congruent with each other. Who am I? __________

Answer Key

Algebra

Exercises

21. Owen has 31 cousins. 17 of his cousins are boys. He wants to figure out how many of his cousins are girls. Which equation represents the situation?

$31 = x \times 17$ $\quad$ $31 = x - 17$ $\quad$ $31 = x + 17$

22. What is the variable in the equation $90 - 10 = r$? __r__

23. Solve for the variable: $24 \div x = 4$ __6__

24. I am an equation that uses the letter z as a variable. I help to find the answer to 90 - 30. Who am I? ____93 – 30 = z____

25. Derek is sailing his ship. He knows that he has gone 130 miles so far. He also knows that he has to sail a total of 189 miles to get where he is going. He wants to know how much further he has to go.

$189 \times 130 = x$ $\quad$ $189 - 130 = x$ $\quad$ $189 + 130 = x$

26. Solve for the variable: $j + 23 = 44$ __21__

27. Ralph is growing pear trees. He has 29 red pear trees and 24 green pear trees. He wants to know how many trees he has all together.

$29 - 24 = y$ $\quad$ $29 \div 24 = y$ $\quad$ $29 + 24 = y$

28. What is the variable in the equation $11 \times 32 = w$? __w__

29. Solve for the variable: $3a = 12$ __a=4__

30. Identify the coefficient: $9y + 18 = 90$ __9__

31. Solve for the variable: $b - 12 = 9$ __21__

32. I am an equation that uses the letter b as a variable. I help to find the answer to 25 + 4. Who am I?
$25 + 4 = b$

33. Solve for the variable: $5x - 10 = 35$ ___9___

34. There are 30 students in your class. You need to split them into 5 teams. Which equation would you use to figure out the students on each team?

$30 - 5 = y$ $30 \div 5 = y$ $30 \times 5 = y$

35. Solve for the variable: $3z + 21 = 51$ ___24___

36. Identify the coefficient: $125y + 100 = 250$ ___125___

37. Solve for the variable: $11x - 12 = 43$ ___5___

38. There are 14 different plants in the garden. Each plant sprouts 8 new buds. Which equation would you use to figure out how many buds you have?

$14 \times 8 = y$ $14 - 8 = y$ $8 - 14 = y$

39. What is the variable in the equation $6p - 25 = 11$? ___p___

40. Solve for the variable: $10x + 2 = 62$ ___6___

Quiz

11. Identify the coefficient in the equation $4t - 3 = 5$ __4__

12. There are 19 fruit trees in Kyle's backyard. 9 of them are apple trees and the rest are peach trees. Which equation represents the situation?

$9x = 19$ $9 - x = 19$ $x + 9 = 19$ (circled)

13. Solve for the variable: $x - 16 = 23$ __7__

14. What is the variable in the equation $17 + r = 74$? __r__

15. Solve for the variable: $3x + 12 = 36$ __8__

16. Identify the coefficient in the equation $20x = 200$ __20__

17. Solve for the variable: $5y - 6 = 14$ __4__

18. There are 8 kittens in a litter. 3 are black and the rest are white. Which equation represents the situation?

$3 - x = 8$ $3 + x = 8$ (circled) $3x = 8$

19. Solve for the variable: $4x = 16$ __4__

20. Solve for the variable: $2x + 9 = 29$ __10__

Data Analysis

Exercises

Clinton is collecting data on the number of yellow leaves on the maple trees near his house. He has his information in a table.

Tree	Number of Yellow Leaves
1	34
2	16
3	28
4	32
5	18
6	34
7	24

21. What is the median for Clinton's data? ____28____

22. What is the range for Clinton's data? ____18____

23. What is the mode for Clinton's data? ____34____

24. What is the mean for Clinton's data? ____26.5____

25. Teddy counts the number of marbles in 8 different bags. (28, 33, 31, 28, 29, 34, 35, 28) What is the mode? ____28____

26. Given the following set, what is the median? (129, 4, -8, 65, -19, 88, 74) ____65____

27. You collect data about the number of movies people have seen in the past month. You get the numbers 2, 0, 4, 1, 6, and 3. What is the median?

______3.5______

28. Karen collects data about the ages of people's pets. She get the numbers 5, 17, 13, 6, 2 and 9. What is the mean?

______8______

29. You collect data on the height of bean plants. You get the numbers 42, 46, 44, 40, 38 and 50. The height of your plant is the same as the median. What is it?

______43______

30. Create a line graph using the following table:

Week	Height of Sunflower
1	5 inches
2	12 inches
3	19 inches
4	23 inches
5	28 inches

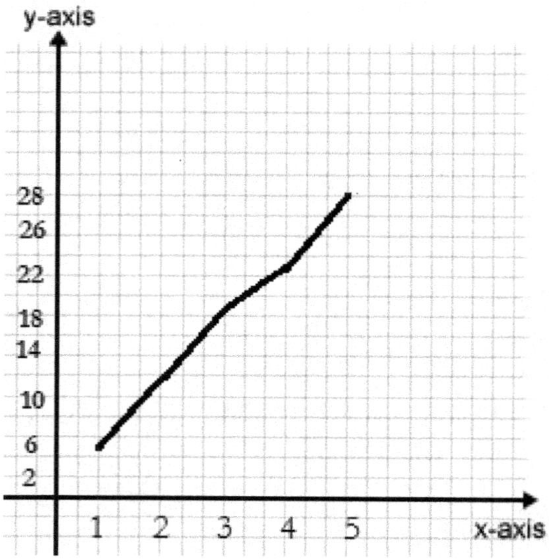

31. Stephen collects data about the pounds of food you eat in a week and get the numbers 17, 20, 23, 19, 16 and 13. If he plotted the line, what direction would it go?

__up and down__

32. Rebecca collects data on the number of pages you read in a day. She gets the numbers 13, 18, 24, 27, 23, 27 and 15. What is the range? ____14____

33. Should John use a survey or observation to collect data on how many nights families sit down and eat dinner together? ____survey____

34. Hector likes to keep a record of how many times he hits a ball at batting practice. (15, 25, 39, 24, 11, 32, 27) What is the mean? ____24.7____

35. Mike practices his saxophone every day. He records the number of minutes he practices for 10 days. Mike wants to know the average number of minutes he practices every day so that he can tell his teacher. (34, 46, 21, 38, 36, 22, 19, 39, 36, 24)

____31.5____

36. Given the following set, what is the mode? (6, 29, 41, 14, 24, 8, 11)

__no mode__

37. Raphael knows how tall seven of his friends are in inches. (60, 64, 69, 62, 66, 59, 61) What is the average height of his friends? ____63____

38. Given the following set, what is the range? (7, 21, 49, 54, 13, 33, 4)

____50____

39. Carla babysits after school. She keeps track of the money that she makes each day so that she can figure out the average amount of money she makes per day. (14, 25, 18, 21, 33)

____22.2____

40. Sam notices his tomato plants are growing at different rates. What is the best way for Sam to figure out how tall his plants are?

a. Measure

Quiz

Daphne is collecting data on the time it takes for her to do homework each night. She has her information in a table.

Night	Time to do Homework
1	22 minutes
2	27 minutes
3	35 minutes
4	27 minutes
5	22 minutes
6	27 minutes
7	16 minutes

11. What is the median for Daphne's data? ____27____

12. What is the range for Daphne's data? ____19____

13. What is the mode for Daphne's data? ____27____

14. What is the mean for Daphne's data? ____25____

15. Should Alyssa use measurement or observation to find the length of driveways in her neighborhood? __measurement__

16. Tracy keeps track of the number of birds who eat at her bird feeder every day for a week. (4, 12, 6, 8, 4, 7, 9) What is the average number of birds who eat at her bird feeder? ____7____

17. Crista loves to run. She keeps track of how many miles she runs over five days. (15, 8, 9, 12, 7) What is the range? ____8____

18. Given the following set of data, what is the mode? (7, 12, 6, 12, 9, 5, 8, 5) ____12 and 5____

19. Eddie reads every night before he goes to bed and keeps track of the number of pages he reads. (34, 29, 12, 18, 25) What is the median? ___25___

20. Create a graph using the following table:

Day	Minutes Practiced the Violin
1	25 minutes
2	20 minutes
3	30 minutes
4	35 minutes
5	40 minutes
6	35 minutes

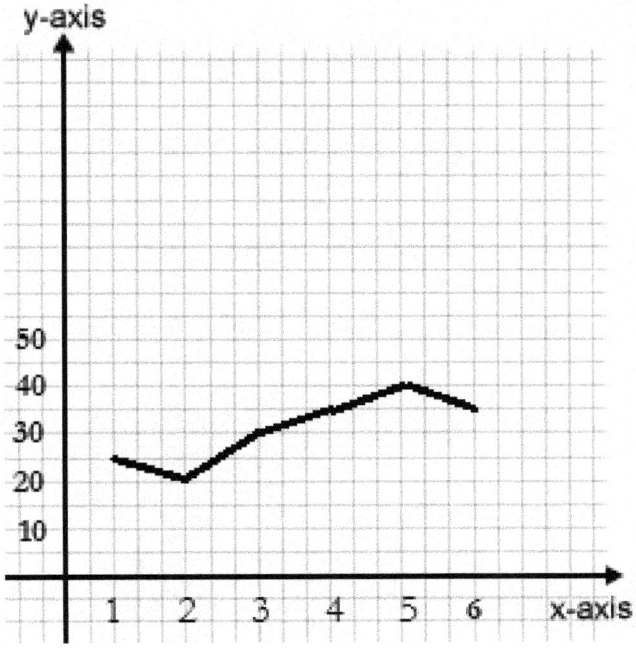

Decimals

Exercises

21. Compare the two numbers: 63.08 > __6.308__

22. Which number is larger? 456354.127 or 456354.129 ___456354.129___

23. What is the value of the number 5 in 3123.95? ___hundredths___

24. Add 43.8 and 127.02 ___170.82___

25. Put the numbers in descending order: 542.8, 512.03, 542.4, 512.72
___542.8, 542.4, 512.72, 512.03___

26. Compare the two numbers: 0.854 > __0.85__

27. 129.45 - 94.031 = ___35.419___

28. Which number is smaller? 4563.483 or 4563.783 ___4563.483___

29. Write the decimal .68 as a fraction ___68/100___

30. What is the value of the number 9 in 934.082? ___hundred___

31. 67.351 + 8.523 = ___75.874___

32. Put the numbers is ascending order: 341.982, 341.985, 349.71, 346.012
___341.982, 341.985, 346.012, 349.71___

33. Which number is larger? 512346.8 or 516346.8 ___516346.8___

34. Compare the two numbers: 2.010 = __2.010__

35. 5.391 - .835 = ___4.556___

36. Put the numbers in ascending order: 1.394, 2.8713, 1.492, 1.842
___1.394, 1.492, 1.842, 2.8713___

37. Which number is smaller? 78.916 or 78.956 ___78.916___

38. Compare the two numbers: 0.11 > __0.111__ ______

39. Write the decimal .451 as a fraction ___451/1000___

40. 78.092 + 498.23 = ___576.322___

Quiz

11. Compare the two numbers: 34.67 > <u>3.467</u>

12. Which number is larger? 587.23 or 587.32 ____587.32____

13. What is the value of the number 3 in 901.234? ____hundredths____

14. Add 219.08 and 76.341 ____295.421____

15. Put the numbers in descending order: 98.342, 98.38, 97.423, 97.03
____98.38, 98.342, 97.423, 97.03____

16. Compare the two numbers: 0.213 < <u>0.22</u>

17. 56.7 – 52.82 = ____3.88____

18. Which number is smaller? 4.623 or .4623 ____.4623____

19. Write the decimal .741 as a fraction ____741/1000____

20. What is the value of the number 4 in 564.87? ____one____

Fractions

Exercises

21. Which fraction is equivalent to $^5/_7$? $^5/_{14}$ $\underline{^{10}/_{14}}$ $^{10}/_{12}$

22. Reduce $^{23}/_3$ ____$7\ ^2/_3$____

23. Which fraction is larger? $\underline{^3/_5}$ or $^4/_{10}$ ________

24. $^5/_8 + ^3/_8 =$ ____1____

25. Find a fraction that is equivalent to 1 ¾ ____$^7/_4$____

26. ½ × $^{13}/_7$ = ____$^{13}/_{14}$____

27. Reduce $^{19}/_5$ ____$3\ ^4/_5$____

28. $^4/_5 - ^3/_{10} =$ ____$^1/_2$____

29. Which fraction is equivalent to $^5/_9$? $^6/_{18}$ $\underline{^{10}/_{18}}$ $^{10}/_{20}$

30. $^{22}/_7 \div ^3/_2 =$ ____$^{44}/_{21}$____

31. Find a fraction that is equivalent to $^6/_7$ ____$^{12}/_{14}$____

32. $^{12}/_{13} - ^5/_{13} =$ ____$^7/_{13}$____

33. $^9/_{14}$ × ½ = ____$^9/_{28}$____

34. Reduce $^{17}/_4$ ____$1\ ^1/_4$____

35. Which fraction is larger? $\underline{^3/_5}$ or $^4/_{10}$

36. $^{15}/_{20} + ^4/_{10} =$ ____$1\ ^3/_{20}$____

37. $^8/_{10} \div ^6/_5 =$ ____$^2/_3$____

38. Find a fraction that is equivalent to $4\ ^7/_9$ ____$^{43}/_9$____

39. $^{14}/_{22} + ^{16}/_{22} =$ ____$^{30}/_{22}$____

40. Reduce $^{50}/_{8}$ $\underline{\quad 6\,^{1}/_{4} \quad}$

Quiz

11. Which fraction is equivalent to $^{9}/_{15}$? $\underline{^{18}/_{30}}$ $^{15}/_{22}$ $^{18}/_{20}$

12. Reduce $^{21}/_{4}$ $\underline{5\ ^{1}/_{4}}$

13. Which fraction is larger? $^{3}/_{6}$ or $\underline{^{7}/_{12}}$ ______

14. $^{6}/_{12} + ^{5}/_{6} =$ $\underline{^{16}/_{12}}$

15. Find a fraction that is equivalent to $2\ ^{3}/_{5}$ $\underline{^{13}/_{5}}$

16. $^{15}/_{4} \times ^{2}/_{9} =$ $\underline{^{5}/_{6}}$

17. Reduce $^{29}/_{6}$ $\underline{4\ ^{5}/_{6}}$

18. $^{5}/_{9} - ^{2}/_{18} =$ $\underline{^{8}/_{18}}$

19. Which fraction is equivalent to $^{6}/_{18}$? $^{7}/_{9}$ $\underline{^{2}/_{6}}$ $^{3}/_{6}$

20. $^{10}/_{12} \div ^{4}/_{9} =$ $\underline{^{90}/_{36}}$

Geometry

Exercises

21. What is the measure of the angle? ____25°____

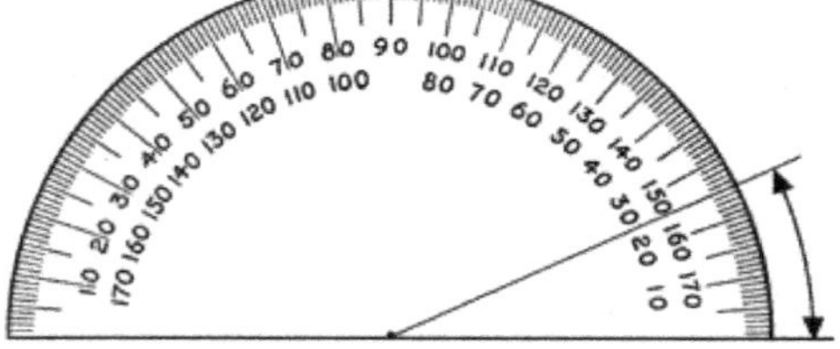

22. What type of angle is this?  ____acute____

23. What type of angle is exactly 90°? ____right____

24. What type of triangle is this? 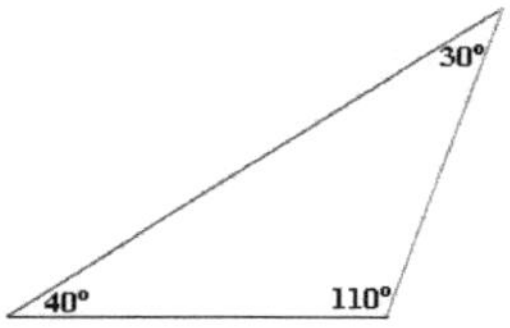

____obtuse____

25. Is this triangle scalene or isosceles? 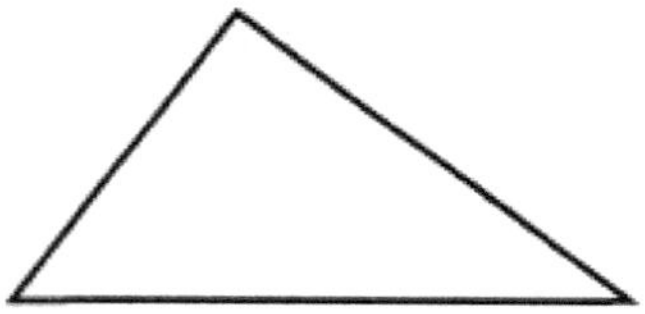 ____scalene____

26. An equilateral triangle has ___3___ equal sides and ___3___ equal angles.

27. What type of triangle is this?  ____isosceles____

28. What are the critical attributes of this pentagon? 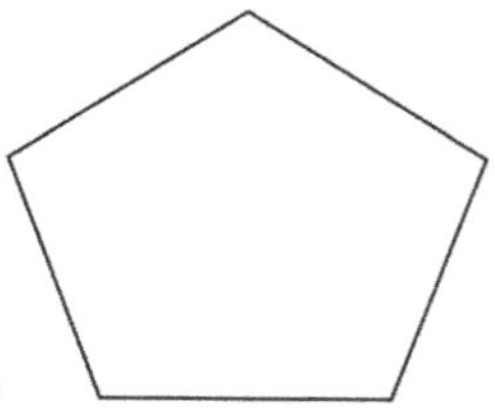 ____5 sides, 5 acute angles and two-dimensional____

29. Which prism is a right prism? 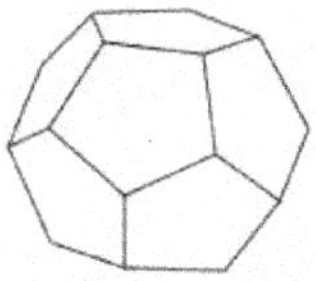 or 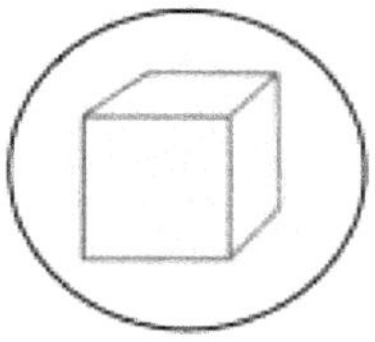

30. What type of pyramid is this? 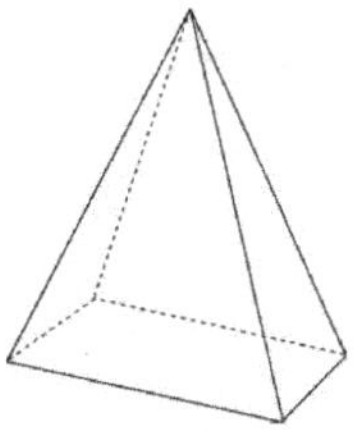 rectangular

31. Which shape has parallel lines and acute angles? 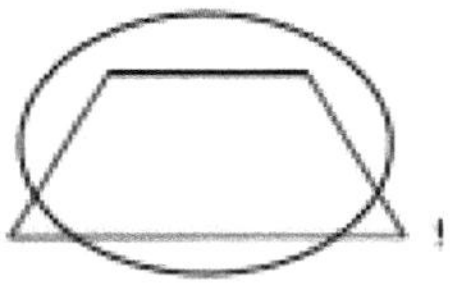 or 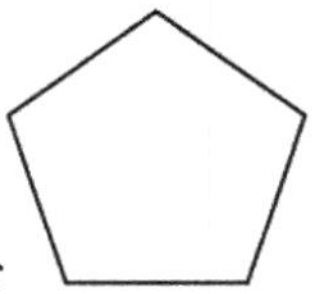

32. Which shape is two-dimensional? 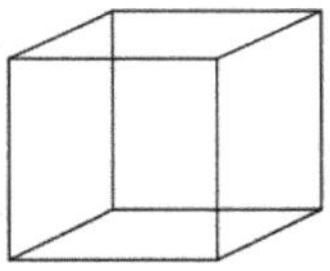 or 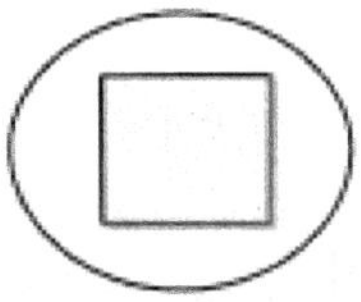

33. What type of triangle is this?  obtuse

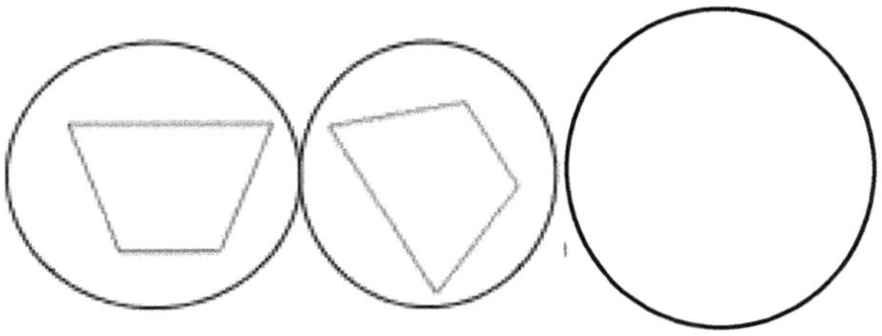

34. Which shapes are congruent?

35. Which shape has three sides, two equal sides and two equal angles? isosceles triangle

36. Which is not three-dimensional? 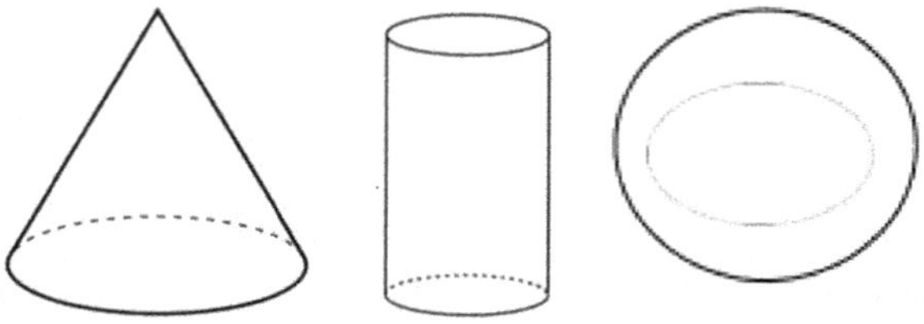

37. What are the measures of the angles in an equilateral triangle? ____60°____

38. Congruent shapes are ____the same size and shape____

39. Which shape does not have a right angle? 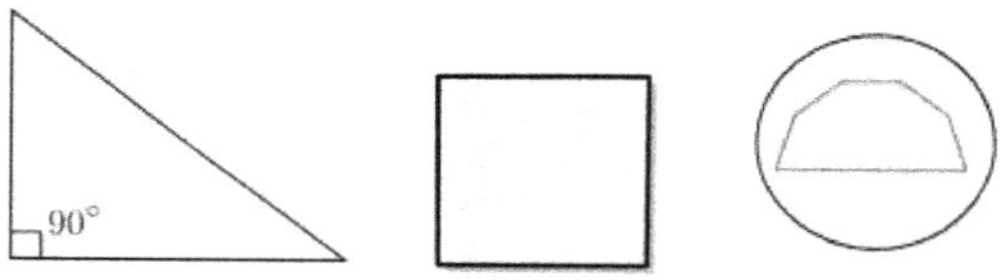

40. An angle that has less than 90° is a ____acute____ angle.

Quiz

11. What is the measure of the angle? ____85°____

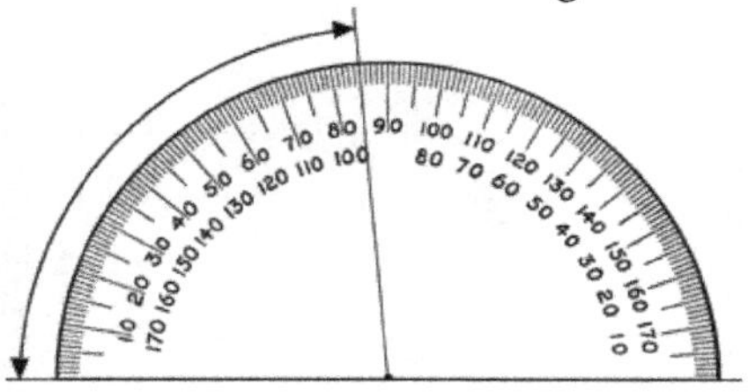

12. What type of angle is this? 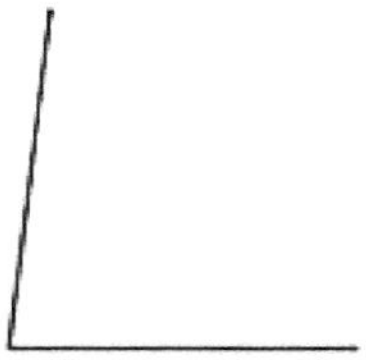 ____acute____

13. What type of angle is exactly 180°? ____straight____

14. What type of triangle is this? 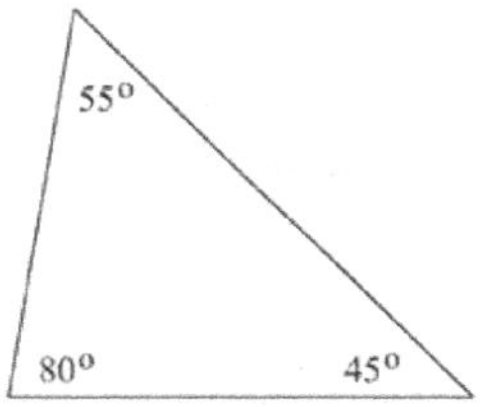

____scalene____

15. Is this triangle scalene or equilateral? 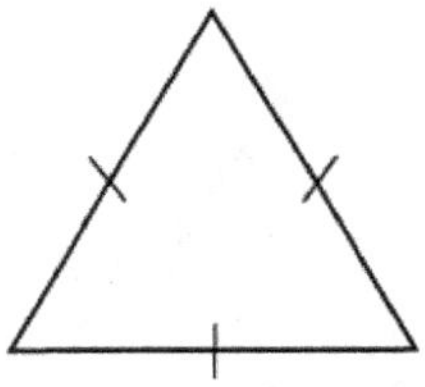 ____equilateral____

16. An isosceles triangle has ____2____ equal sides and ____2____ equal angles.

17. What type of triangle is this? 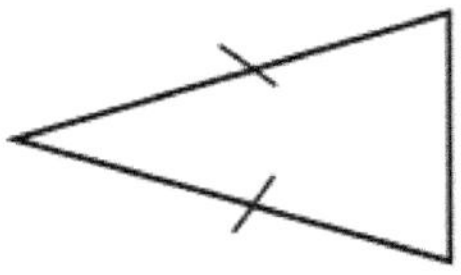 ____isosceles____

18. What are the critical attributes of this hexagon? 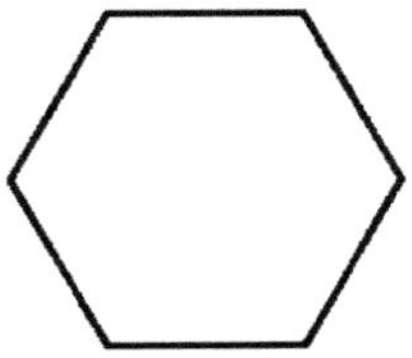 ____6 sides, 6 acute angles and two-dimensional____

19. Which prism is a hexagonal pyramid? 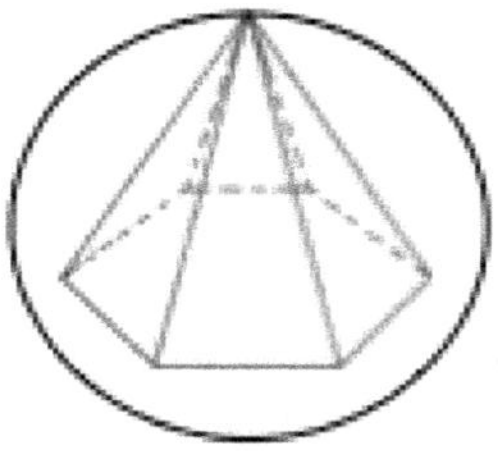 or 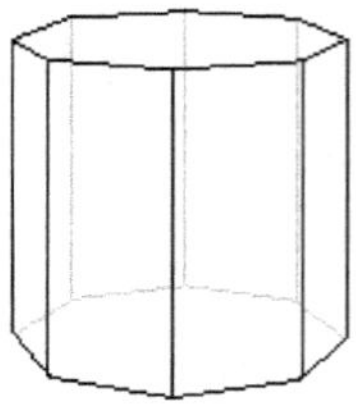

20. Which shape is not three-dimensional? 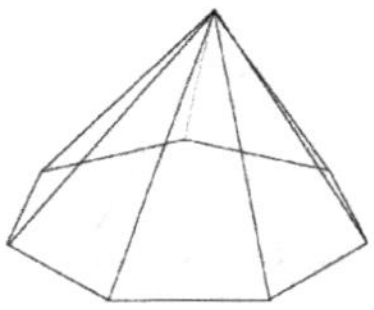 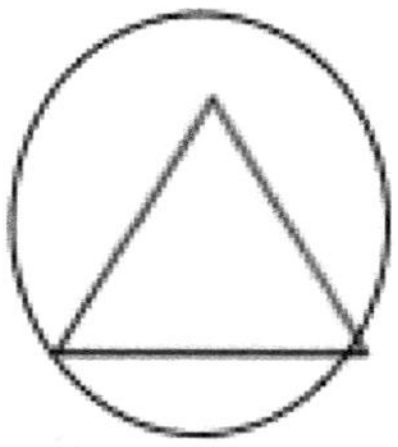 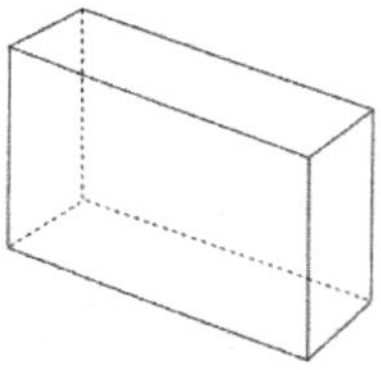

Measurement

Exercises

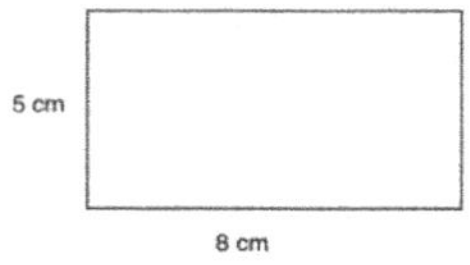

21. Figure out the area of the rectangle. ______40 cm^2______

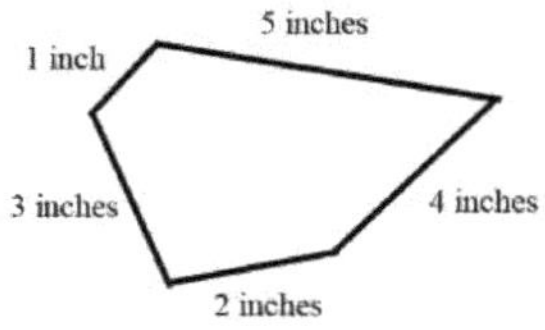

22. What is the perimeter of the pentagon? ____15 inches____

23. Convert 1500 milliliters to liters. ______1.5 liters______

24. How many centimeters are in 1.42 meters? ______142______

25. What temperature is displayed on the thermometer in Fahrenheit?

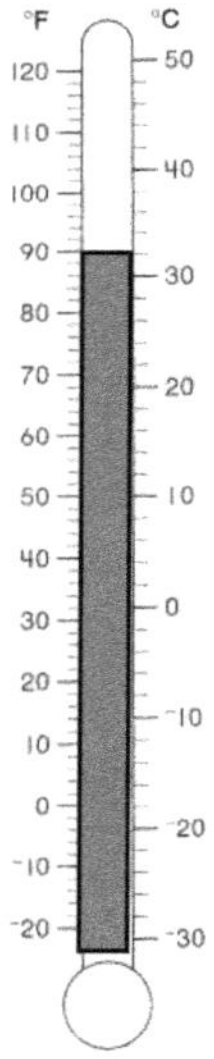

____88°____

26. How many hours pass between 8:45AM and 2:15PM?____5 ½ hours ____

27. How many kilometers are there in 2000 meters? ________2________

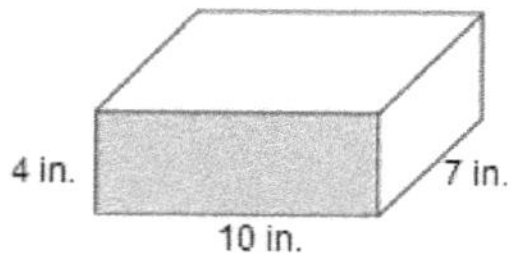

28. Find the volume of the prism. ____280 $inches^3$____

29. Convert 24 inches to feet. ____2 feet____

30. What is the temperature difference between 45 degrees Celsius and 17 degrees Celsius?
____28 degrees____

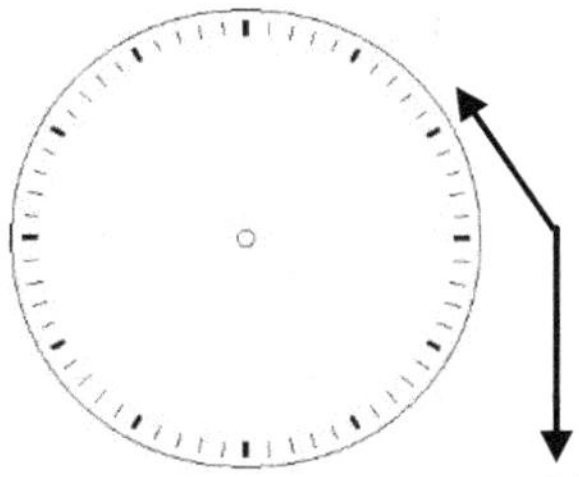

31. What time is it? ____10:31____

32. What is the perimeter of the octagon that has all equal sides measuring 5 meters?
____40 meters____

33. How many meters are in 24 kilometers? ____24000____

34. What is the area of a rectangle that has a length of 8 meters and a width of 12 meters?
____96 meters^2____

35. Convert 900 centimeters to meters. ____9 meters____

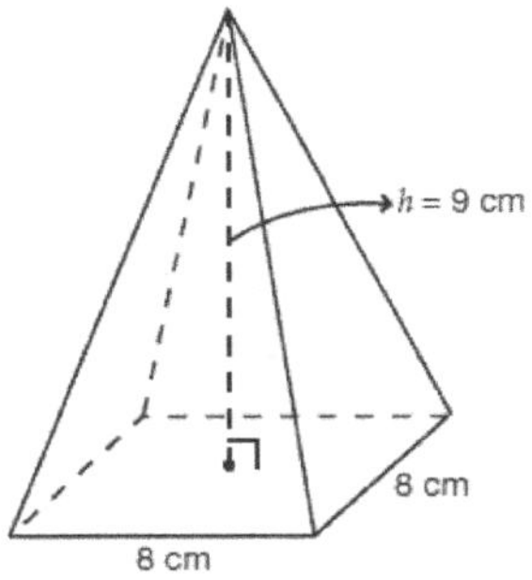

36. Find the volume of the pyramid. ____576 cm^3____

37. How many hours pass between 11PM and 6:45AM? ____7 ¾ hours____

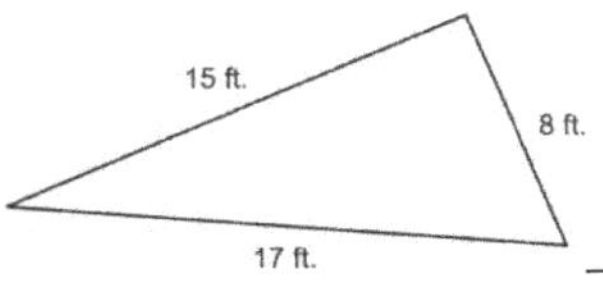

38. What is the perimeter of the triangle? ____40 feet____

39. What is the temperature difference between 13 degrees Celsius and 31 degrees Celsius?
____18 degrees____

40. Convert 8020 centimeters to kilometers. _____.0802____

Quiz

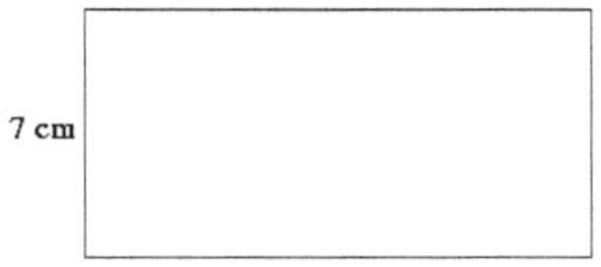

11. Figure out the area of the rectangle. ___98 cm^2___

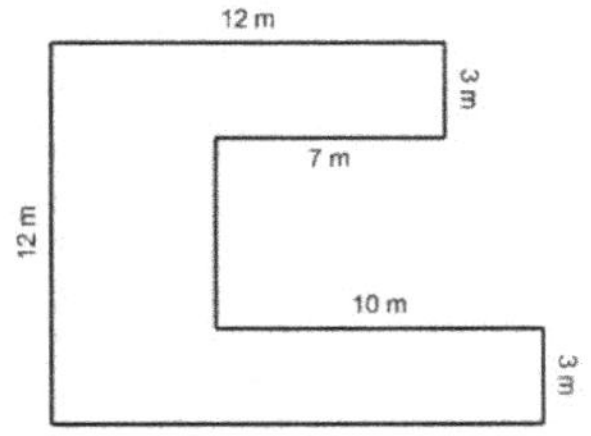

12. What is the perimeter of the polygon? ___62 meters___

13. Convert 1.2 liters to milliliters. ___1200___

14. How many centimeters are in 3.46 meters? ___346___

15. What temperature is displayed on the thermometer in Fahrenheit?

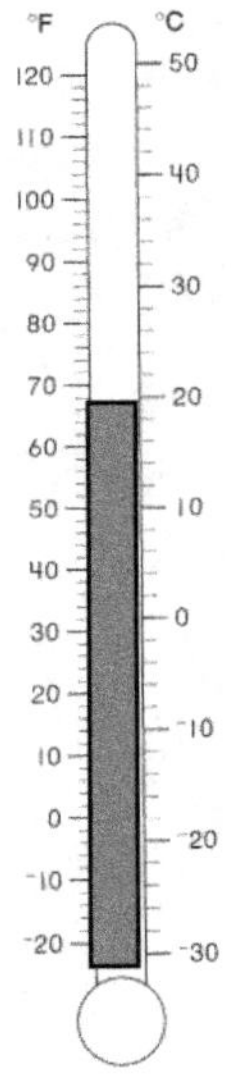

___66°___

16. How many hours pass between 3:15PM and 2:30AM? ___6 ¼ hours___

17. How many kilometers are there in 5600 meters? ___5.6___

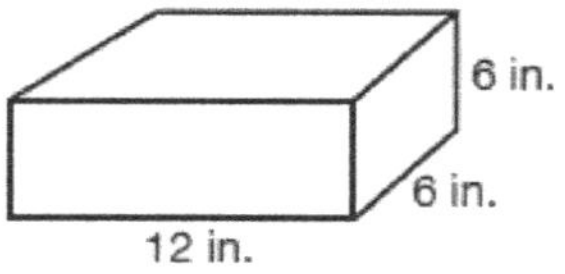

18. Find the volume of the prism. ______$432\ in^3$______

19. Convert 21 feet to yards. ______7 yards______

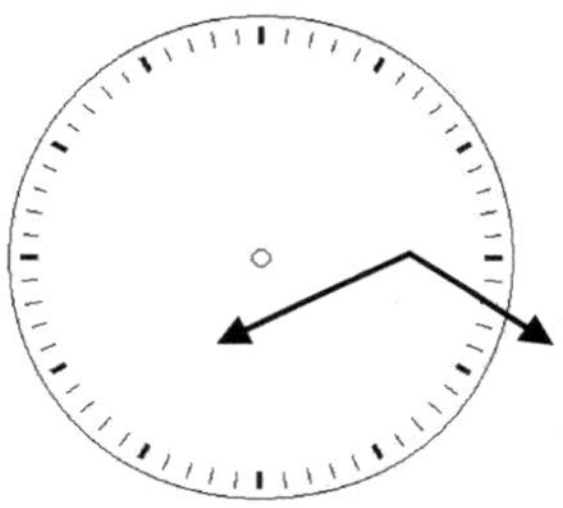

20. What time is it? ______4:41______

Multiplying Large Numbers

Exercises

1. 452 × 3 = 1356

2. 843 × 7 = 5901

3. 1294 × 5 = 6470

4. 789 × 6 = 4734

5. 1370 × 8 = 10960

6. 6208 × 6 = 37248

7. 1275 × 12 = 15300

8. 5714 × 31 = 177134

9. 1982 × 18 = 35676

10. 567 × 23 = 13041

11. 871 × 24 = 20904

12. 8113 × 44 = 356972

13. 3012 × 11 = 33132

14. 3124 × 121 = 378004

15. 1286 × 307 = 394802

16. 7823 × 202 = 1580246

17. 4506 × 247 = 1112982

18. 6062 × 314 = 1903468

19. 2879 × 403 = 1160237

20. 9126 × 321 = 2929446

Quiz

1. 583
× 7

4081

2. 719
× 4

2876

3. 2013
× 3

6039

4. 827
× 15

12405

5. 4099
× 18

73782

6. 1753
× 24

42072

7. 2591
× 347

899077

8. 1277
× 233

297541

9. 874
× 503

439622

10. 6183
×782

4835106

Probability

Exercises

21. If there are 8 colors on a color wheel, what is the probability of landing on each individual color?
    1/8

22. What is the probability, in a percentage, of 3/8? 37.5%

23. If there is a 2/5 chance of something happening, what is the likelihood that it will happen?
    unlikely

24. There is a 1/6 chance that you will roll a 1, 2, 3, 4, 5, or 6 when rolling a dice. What is the probability that you will roll an odd number? 1/2

25. Place the following probability outcomes on the probability line: 1/9, 5/9, 9/9

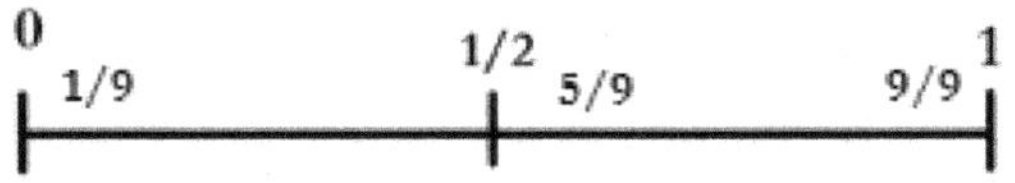

26. There are 14 baseballs in the bag, 9 footballs, 5 soccer balls and 18 tennis balls. List all of the possible outcomes for the type of ball that one could get when reaching into the bag.
    baseball 14/46 football 9/46
    soccer 5/46
    tennis 18/46

27. If there is a 25% chance of rain, what is the likelihood that it will rain?
    not likely

28. There are 15 marbles in a jar with an equal number of pink, teal and purple marbles. What is the probability of getting a pink marble? 1/3

29. What is the probability, in a percentage, of 7/11? 63%

30. There is a 1/5 chance of choosing a brownie, cookie, slice of pie, slice of cake or pudding. What is the probability that you will choose a slice of something?
    2/5

31. There are 6 compliments are written on pink pieces of paper, 11 compliments are written on blue pieces of paper and 8 compliments are written white pieces of paper in a compliment jar. List all of the possible outcomes for the color paper that one will get when reaching into the jar to pull out a compliment.
    pink- 6/25
    blue- 11/25
    white- 8/25

32. There are 16 clownfish, 23 angelfish, 11 anemone and 19 seahorses in an aquarium. Which fish are you most likely to get if you reach in?

angelfish

33. If there is a 80% chance that you will pass a test, what is the likelihood of passing?

likely

34. Place the following probability outcomes on the probability line: 3/15, 7/15, 14/15

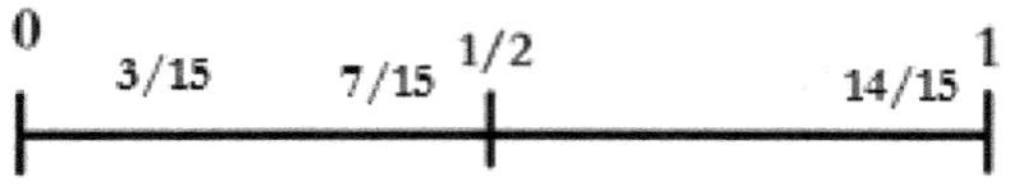

35. There are 36 pets in the shelter. Half are dogs and 1/3 are cats. What is the probability you will choose a cat? _12/36_

36. What is the probability, in a percentage, of 9/27 _33%_

37. There are 26 daisies, 13 roses, 17 irises, and 23 carnations in one container. What is the probability that you will pull out a rose when you reach in the container?

_13/79_

38. If there is a 48% chance of winning the game, what is the likelihood that you will win the game?

even chance

39. There are 11 chocolate donuts, 17 plain donuts and 22 glazed donuts in a box. List all of the possible outcomes for the type of donut that one will get when taking one out of the box.

chocolate- 11/50

plain- 17/50

glazed- 22/50

40. There are 62 cans of paint. 24 are white, 17 are pink and the rest are purple. What is the probability you will choose a purple can? _21/62_

Quiz

11. If there are 12 colors on a color wheel, what is the probability of landing on each individual color?
__1/12__

12. What is the probability, in a percentage, of 6/14? __43%__

13. If there is a 4/8 chance of something happening, what is the likelihood that it will happen?
even chance

14. There is a 1/6 chance that you will roll a 1, 2, 3, 4, 5, or 6 when rolling a dice. What is the probability that you will roll a number less than 4? __1/2__

15. Place the following probability outcomes on the probability line: 0/7, 4/7, 6/7

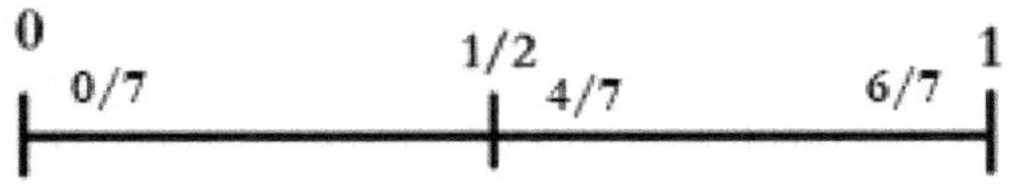

16. Mark has different uniforms for his job. He has 7 white shirts, 9 blue shirts and 12 striped shirts. List all of the possible outcomes for the type of shirt that Mark could get when he reaches in his uniform drawer.

    ______white- 7/28______
    ______blue- 9/28______
    ______striped- 12/28______

17. If there is a 85% chance of rain, what is the likelihood that it will rain?
__likely__

18. There are 25 marbles in a jar with an equal number of orange, blue, white, green and yellow marbles. What is the probability of getting an orange marble?
__1/5__

19. What is the probability, in a percentage, of 6/18? __33%__

20. There is a 1/6 chance of getting a vanilla, chocolate, twist, raspberry, peanut butter or blackberry ice cream cone. What is the probability that you will choose a berry flavored ice cream cone?
__2/6__

Whole Numbers

Exercises

21. Is 9 a prime or composite number? composite

22. Round the answer to 92 + 16 110

23. What are the factors pairs for 24? 1 and 24, 2 and 12, 3 and 8, 4 and 6

24. What is the value of 7 in the number 821,734? hundred

25. Estimate the answer to 88 ÷ 9 10

26. Write the number 682 in expanded form 600 + 80 + 2

27. Round the answer to 116 – 43 80

28. Is 23 a prime or composite number? prime

29. What are the factor pairs for 30? 1 and 30, 2 and 15, 3 and 10, 5 and 6

30. Write the number 430 in written form four hundred thirty

31. Estimate the answer to 103 × 5 500

32. Round the answer to 73 + 29 100

33. What are the factors of 66? 1 ,2, 3, 6, 11, 22, 33, 66

34. What is the value of 3 in the number 9,302,145? hundred thousand

35. Write the number 7832 in expanded form 7000 + 800 + 30 + 2

36. Round the answer to 93 – 12 80

37. Is 86 prime or composite? composite

38. Estimate the answer to 67 + 43 + 19 130

39. What are the factor pairs for 40? 1 and 40, 2 and 20, 4 and 10, 5 and 8

40. What is the value of 5 in the number 8,645,023? thousand

Quiz

11. Is 15 a prime or composite number? composite

12. Round the answer to 97 ÷ 5 20

13. What are the factors pairs for 32? 1 and 32, 2 and 16, 4 and 8

14. What is the value of 2 in the number 298,539? hundred thousand

15. Estimate the answer to 34 + 15 + 89 140

16. Write the number 989 in expanded form 900 + 80 + 9

17. Round the answer to 832 – 513 300

18. Is 31 a prime or composite number? prime

19. What are the factor pairs for 42? 1 and 42, 2 and 21, 3 and 14, 6 and 7

20. Write the number 781 in written form seven hundred eighty one

Word Problems

Exercises

21. Jeremy is spending his summer mowing lawns. He has 13 different lawns that he is responsible for mowing. He gets paid $12 for each lawn that he mows. Week 1, Jeremy mows 6 lawns. How much does he make? ____$72____

22. Carrie loves to scrapbook. She uses stickers to help make her scrapbook pages more colorful. Carrie uses about 4 stickers per page. There are 18 pages in Carrie's scrapbook. Estimate how many stickers she used in her scrapbook?

    ____80____

23. Roger goes fishing. He catches 15 bass. He likes to share his fish with his friends. He divides his fish between 5 people. Write an equation and then solve to figure out how many fish each person will get. __x = 3__

24. I am three-dimensional. I have no right angles, no parallel lines and no perpendicular lines. I could roll. Who am I? __sphere__

25. Justin fixes heaters. When he gets to a house with no heat he takes the temperature. He measured the temperature as 63.8°. After he fixed the heater and the heat went on, he measured the temperature as 72.9°. How much did the temperature rise? _9.1 degrees

26. You have a friend who moves to Hawaii. It is 7:13 at night and you really want to call your friend to talk to him. His time zone is 3 hours behind yours. What time is it where your friend is?

    ____4:13____

27. There are three color plates that are used in the cafeteria. There are 100 yellow plates, 50 green plates and 50 blue plates. What is the probability that you will get a green plate?

    ____1/4____

28. There are 90 dresses. You have tried on $^1/_4$ of them. Write an equation and then solve to figure out how many dresses you have tried on. _x = 22.5__

29. Ralph has a toy that is a regular hexagon. The sides are an even number. He figures out that the perimeter of the hexagon is 24 inches, but he wants to know how long each of the sides are.

    __6 inches_

30. I am three-dimensional. I have 2 pairs of parallel lines and 4 right angles. My faces meet at one point on top. Who am I? __pyramid_

31. Pat loves to play sports. He has a bag of balls in his garage. There are 14 baseballs in the bag, 9 footballs, 5 soccer balls and 18 tennis balls. List all of the possible outcomes for the type of ball that Pat could get when he reaches in his bag.

baseballs- 14/46, footballs- 9/46, soccer- 5/46, tennis- 18/46

32. There are 38 spoons to be washed. You have done half. Write an equation and then solve to figure out the total number of spoons you washed.

x = 19

33. Sally needs to know the volume of a container that is 14 centimeters tall. The length and width are half of the height. What is the volume? 686 cm^3

34. Mr. Smith is making brownies for his class. He is making two batches. The original recipe calls for 1/3 cup of oil. How much oil does he need now?

2/3 cup

35. Sebastian, Hank, Theresa and Josie all kept track of the snowfall in their city for the month of January. Sebastian's city got 35.269 inches of snow in January. Hank's city got 5 thousandths more than Sebastian's city. How much snow did his city get?

35.274

36. Which shape has 4 sides of different lengths, 4 right angles and is two dimensional?

polygon

37. Joe is playing a ball pit. There are 78 yellow balls, 93 red balls and 84 blue balls. What is the probability that he will pick up a yellow ball when he reaches all the way down to the bottom of the ball pit? 78/255

38. Sebastian, Hank, Theresa and Josie all kept track of the snowfall in their city for the month of January. Sebastian's city got 35.269 inches of snow in January. Theresa's city got 4.02 more inches of snow than Hank's city. How much snow did her city get?

39.289

39. Jaclyn babysits 3 days a week. She makes $11 an hour. If she babysat for 9 hours one week, how much money did she make? $99

40. Tim shops and buys items that cost $6.78, $11.32 and $23.45. Round the cost of the items to figure how about how much he will spend. $44

Quiz

11. Ilene is an artist. She makes ceramic bowls and sells them at craft fairs. Ilene has 27 bowls to bring with her to the craft fair on Saturday. At the craft fair, Ilene sells all of her bowls. Ilene also gets orders for 19 bowls. It takes Ilene 3 hours to make each bowl. How long will it take her to make the bowls that were ordered? __57 hours__

12. Henry is helping at a spaghetti dinner. He is in charge of making the juice. Henry has to use 13 gallons of water to make the juice every half an hour. After 3 hours, estimate how many gallons of water will Henry have used?

__30 gallons__

13. Pam loves to paint. She has 56 different color paints. Pam wants to put her paints in containers. The containers only hold 8 colors each. Write an equation and then solve to figure out how many containers will Pam need?

__x = 7__

14. You are learning to scuba dive. You start in waters that are 62.6° As you start to dive down the water gets colder. It is 11.7° colder where you dive than it is at the surface. What is the temperature of the water you are diving in?

__50.9 degrees__

15. You are timing a race. The first person passes the finish line in 23 minutes and 16 seconds. The last person passes the finish line in 37 minutes and 29 seconds. How much faster was the first person than the last person?

__14 minutes and 13 seconds__

16. Your teacher has 5 different types of stickers that she puts on completed homework. She has 15 smiley faces, 20 flowers, 20 hearts, 15 stars and 25 animals. What is the probability that you will get a heart sticker on your paper?

__20/95__

17. There are 58 photos printed. You have to print 3 times more. Write an equation and then solve to figure out how many photos total you have to print.

__x = 174__

18. Kyle is planning a senior prank. He is going to cover the football field with spray paint. He knows the area of a field is 121 meters^2. The sides of the field are the same. Kyle needs to know what the lengths of the sides of the field are so that he can make sure he has enough people on each side to get the field completely covered. __11 meters__

19. Kristie is making cookies for a surprise party. There will be a lot of people there so Kristie needs to triple the recipe. The original recipe calls for ½ tsp. baking soda. How much baking soda does Kristie need now? __1 ½ tsp._

20. I am three-dimensional. I have 6 faces and 6 pairs of parallel lines. Each face has right angles. All of my faces are congruent with each other. Who am I?

__cube__

CPSIA information can be obtained
at www.ICGtesting.com
Printed in the USA
LVHW062306200320
650778LV00008B/98

9 781629 170756